HOW TO TALK DIRTY

A Hands-on Guide to Phone Sex

Jenny Ainslie-Turner

House of Erotica

An imprint of
Andrews UK Limited

Published by House of Erotica
An imprint of Andrews UK Limited
The Hat Factory
Bute Street
Luton
LU1 2EY
www.houseoferoticabooks.com

Published in association with Cambridge House Ltd
Suite 7, Mayden House
Long Bennington Business Park
Newark, NG23 5DJ

ISBN 978-1-84989-663-4

Printed and bound in the UK by CPI UK, Croydon

A catalogue record of this book
is available from the British Library

Contents

Jenny Ainslie-Turner is a phone sex veteran and star of Channel 4's 'My Phone Sex Secrets'.

This is her story.

HOW TO TALK DIRTY

A Hands-on Guide to Phone Sex

No Subject Taboo, Taste The Forbidden

All our adverts inform the prospective caller of this; No Subject Taboo, Taste The Forbidden, irrespective of the main heading. There again, so do a few other companies in the 'call back' phone sex business. We, on the other hand, stand by our word. We do actually speak about anything. No matter if it is taboo. We cater to every fantasy. This is the reality of the live phone sex or adult chat lines.

Some of these subject matters are areas of great interest to some men. And, curiosity is really all it is. For some, their frustration haunts them daily until they are able to set their demons free, and the only way to do this safely, is to talk to someone who understands their need to talk openly about their hang-ups, and even to go as far as helping them to fulfil their fantasies, obsessions, fetishes or whatever it is you like to call them.

Many of the guys or callers, as I refer to them. After all, that's what they are, actually feel quite guilty about their particular fantasy and say as much. Most are not even aware how common their fantasies are. They range from having sex with their sister or auntie to their mother-in-law, even their mothers. On the odd occasion, even their mother and father!

Some fantasise about their wives or girlfriends having sex with other men, either willingly or against their will. The most common fantasy of all is sex with a teenager. Again, it's something they can never have and you know what they say about forbidden fruits!

Whatever their reason, fetish, fantasy or obsession, they need and will always need women like me to set them free of their tormenting demons so they can go about their daily lives rid of the evil that secretly lies within them. This desperate need they have which is so often suppressed is what makes Live Call Back companies and Premium Rate Lines such a popular, thriving industry.

However, there is a lighter side to the darkness that hides within the heart of man. A lightness that will shine throughout the pages of my book as I recount the tales of men who regularly call me, in the hope of fulfilling their 'Darkest Desires.'

Chapter One

Where Did It All Begin?

"Hello. Live call back....."

This is how my day always starts for me. Could be 5am. Could be, on a bad day, 5pm. One thing's for sure, the days or nights are never boring, nor are they ever predictable.

"Can you give me some details, please?" More often than not, would come the reply. Or sometimes a timid, "How much is it for a call?"

My initial reply is always the same. "We've got girls from sixteen to seventy-three. And we do talk about anything. Do you want to know the price to your land line or to your mobile?"

We didn't really have all those girls. "We," are just little me. From 'Amber' sixteen, to 'Mable' seventy-three there is only ever me. And, when called for, *I* do the two-girl calls. Providing they are not the same age, that is. I've been found out a couple of times but it is only to be expected. They are not all morons, well not all the time.

If it's a guy I've had several times in the same day I might hear;

"Are you the girl I've just spoken to on reception?"

"No!" I vehemently reply. "I wish I was," I tell them. "She's ten years younger than me (or twenty years younger

3

if I'm pretending to be sixty.)" I sound so indignant at their suggestion that the idea is put right out of their heads. However, if they still insist that I'm one and the same, I usually give in and say. "She's my sister." Yeah, right. I'm an only child.

Astoundingly, I've been as many as twenty different girls to some of my regulars, one of which I've been having for over a year, now. Not only that, I've been four different girls on reception when he's rung through to book a call. His phone number which I obviously know off by heart shows on my hand set. We don't accept withheld numbers. He still hasn't a clue, well, that's not completely true. He did once or twice suspect I'd given him the same sixteen year old a couple of times, but he was never quite sure. He's been one of the most difficult ones to do as different girls, as it goes. Mainly, because I know off by heart his particular fantasy; two fat girls having a cat fight. Now, he's settled on Chrissie, I make certain she gives him the best call. The fantasy always starts the same in a hot sweaty room and we are always on 'our time of the month.' He likes very detailed descriptions; everything from what we are wearing on our feet to our long dangly earrings, then we proceed to knock the shit out of each other, quite literally. Shit, blood, piss and sweat is what turns him on. Surprisingly, he's not the only one; I have several others with similar fantasies. Maybe he's coming through to me in disguise, also. So, as I was saying, he's one of the hardest to do, because there's only so many ways you can do a cat fight.

One of my regulars summed it all up for me one time when I was doing a call with him, this is how it's termed, 'doing a call' with all call back companies. He said it was the best form of sexual release he knows without actually having to climb out of bed. And if you're going to do a fantasy, well it might as well be the most perverted ever imaginable, even unimaginable!

Now, for those of you who don't know; a Call back company, which is what I am, is completely different to premium rate lines. You know, the 0906/0909 numbers. You've seen the adverts in all the Newspapers and Men's magazines. Some are advertised as chat lines others party lines, these are basically the same, soft chat lines. More accessible to all ages, however, only eighteen and above can use them. These calls are paid for by the callers land line phone bill. We, on the other hand, take payment by credit/debit card, cheque and postal order. We mainly advertise in an adult orientated daily newspaper. Along with the men's magazines, occasionally, but we are tucked away in the Classifieds in both paper and magazine. With us you have to book a call for a stated length of time and this is paid for when you book the call. Which will be terminated at that given time, either ten, fifteen, twenty minutes or however long the guy wants the call for. It can even be an open call lasting up to three hours, which I myself have done. As I said, we call you back. Hence the term Call Back.

The guy rings through, asks for details, we give the name of girls we've got on at the moment, (me). We always ask the age group they're interested in. No foreign girls, though. I can't do accents. I can do posh bitch, schoolgirl, granny, dirty slapper, demure, bossy, northern, and southern. These are all the voices I can do. I can be cute or a bit dim. I can be submissive or dominating. I can be fat, thin, tall, short, small tits, big tits, hairy or shaven. A blonde, a redhead and a brunette. Thankfully, all this lot sounds the same. But most of all, I'm never me! On reception I'm Dee Dee. This name came about from my first ever advert 'Darkest Desires.' I took the initials DD and so, Dee Dee, was born. Dee Dee herself, however, was born out of 'Jolene, a fiery redhead who loves talking dirty.' Dee Dee's description is exactly the same. 'Jolene' was who I was on the premium rate lines, when I first started out.

'We' are, Jolene and Dee Dee, five foot six, long wavy dark red hair, green eyes, dress size sixteen and a thirty-six 'C' cup bra. For some reason guys seem to love this size. This is a pity, really, because I'm not. I'm closer to size twenty-two. And I'm not a redhead. However, on the phone I can be whoever I want to be and this is what I love the most about this job. That and making the callers make a sticky mess of themselves. I find it liberating, somehow. Like having control over them and of course, give them a real good dirty time. I just love getting them all out of control and hearing them becomes all unnecessary over the phone. Sometimes it takes just seconds, we all know about those, don't we girls. Some do take a bit of effort and imagination. Well, I do like a challenge and some of them are very challenging to say the least!

As I was saying earlier, one of my regular callers once summed it up for me.

'What's the point of doing a fantasy if it's not as dirty and outrageous as it can be? Something you wouldn't dream of doing in reality. You can do the normal every day sex, every day. But with a fantasy you can let your imagination run wild.'

And with him I do. Another bonus, he sussed me out. Took him long enough, mind. It took him from mid November to mid April to realise all the women he spoke to were one and the same; me. In that time he spoke with seventeen different girls, I checked out the record card I have on him. Oh yes, I keep a record of every guy I've ever spoke to through my company and all the stuff they talk about. Well, you have to, sometimes it can be six or even nine months before they call again and I need to know the sort of chat they're into. I'd hate to give them the wrong girl! The girls he's had are from Tracy aged sixteen to Mary aged sixty-three. He always started with the same question.

"What's the dirtiest thing you've ever done?"

He tested my skills of invention to the limit, luckily for me it was never the same age group when he came through. Sometimes a forty to fifty year old or even sixty to seventy year old and maybe now and again a sixteen year old. Goodness only knows how dirty a sixteen year old can ever be, I'll never know. All the guys come on expecting a sixteen year old to be as experienced as a fifty year old. Sorry guys, they just don't exist. None of the call backs employ sixteen years olds, they're too busy enjoying themselves to talk to perverts on the phone. Bless them, still they can at least fantasise and that's what it's all about.

I remember this one guy asking if we'd got any sixteen year olds on our books.

"Only I called this one company and she sounded like a forty-six not sixteen." He informed me.

I chuckled, "I can probably guess which company it was, but I'm not saying anything."

"No, nor am I," he chuckled.

"I have a lovely young girl called Becky," I tell him with all the conviction I can muster. So he tried Becky, sweet little Becky, who's not so innocent. Well, I guess he must have enjoyed her; he called me back and said how good she was. To which I replied.

"She's such a little minx, very popular with the guys." And so I should be, it's what I get paid a lot of money for.

I've got at least three dozen regulars to whom I'm a sixteen year old. If they know it's the same girl, they don't say. Well, it is just fantasy, after all. You could say I'm fantasizing about being sixteen, again. For the most part they always talk about the same fantasy. Each guy has his own particular fantasy and more often than not it's the same scenario. In the Schoolgirl fantasy, I'm a dirty little schoolgirl teasing the men. The thing is with a fantasy, you can be as dirty and disgusting as you want to be but, and it's a big important '*but*,' it is all in the mind. Just as well, really, because with some of them it's the best place for them, in the recess of their depraved tiny minds.

Amazingly, as it seems, I've had the same guys phoning me for over two years. And yes, we did talk about anything, But you never mentioned the word, except. Well, I could say what I liked; after all, it was my company. Besides, it's standard practice with all the call back companies. If a caller got on to a subject which was taboo like underage or incest, or even animals there was always a way around it. We do touch on those subjects, slightly. Incest was usually with my cousin and your cousin isn't illegal. Underage, well, I always talk about me seeing my first erect cock when I caught my little brother's school mate masturbating in our toilet. He was aged twelve and I was thirteen and a half. That covered underage. Animals, well I always talk about my friend's dog trying to shag my leg. Let's face it, dogs and men are all dirty little bastards!

Mind you, some guy's incest fantasy is with his Mother or Auntie, sometimes even their Father. I'm talking about grown men talking about sex with their parents. I remember chatting with one of my regulars about his particular fantasy; he was into fantasising about an incestuous relationship with his mother. He told me one time it wasn't his actual biological mother he fantasised about. It was me, being his mother that turned him on.

Over the years, I've discovered a lot of things about men, their fantasies and how they've come about and most important of all is, that's just what they are, flights of fancy. I never question nor do I laugh at their particular fantasy or fetish no matter how extreme or bizarre. I help them the best

I can to fulfil it. I enjoy giving them sexual relief. More often than not they get me off, too. Oh, yes, for me it's not just one way street. Of course I fake it from time to time but on the whole I enjoy it every bit as much as they do, provided it's something I'm into that is.

A great example of it only being fantasy is a regular of mine whose into golden showers - wants me to pee on him. Sometimes I go to the loo so he can hear me pee. He absolutely gets off on that big time. He talks a great deal about my pissy knickers and even went as far as asking to buy a pair of them. I asked, as I always do, what he wanted on them. (Oh yes, you'd be surprised what they want on them!) I enquired if he wanted me to pee in them. 'God, no!' he replied chuckling. Then went on to explain 'That's just the fantasy, my dear, all I want on them is the smell of your lovely pussy.'

Yes, from time to time I do chat with them about their particular fantasies. Some callers actually feel the need to explain their particular fantasy. Some want you to fulfil it down to the finest detail, especially the domination calls. This is what I do, am still doing to this day; fulfilling their deepest darkest desires.

However, this is not how I started out. Me being a 1-2-1 chat girl, started several years ago. All my friends who knew me all said the same. I was made for the job and, I guess, they were right. I am perfect for the job. Some, myself included, said all my life and experiences had been heading towards this line of work right from the age of twenty-one. Almost thirty years ago. Although to several dozen Toms, Dicks (quite literally) and Harrys I am any age between sixteen and seventy-three.

When I split with my second husband of eleven years. I lost everything, from my job, my friends to my lovely home in a beautiful picturesque village, in Hadrian's Country where I loved living with my two black Labradors. All this is now a distant memory of happier times spent there.

Then, if that wasn't enough, during a visit back in my home town of Newley, my elderly Mother suffer a near fatal heart attack and I had to stay and care for her. Which in a way was a godsend I suppose, because I had nowhere else to go and thankfully, since the heart attack, she's never been better in her life.

At that time however, I was out of work, caring for Mum. I had to go on benefits. I was forty-six years old and had worked full time all my life since the age of fourteen. We'd always struggled, my ex and I, but no more than anyone else. Now, every single penny was precious. Poor old Ma, used to help as much as she could which wasn't much. After all, she was just a pensioner herself. My Ma and I struggled this way for almost a year. Then, one night, all that changed, not straightaway you understand but it started a chain of events that would completely change my entire life forever and for the better in more ways than I ever could have dreamt of.

I was sat this particular night, bored out my tiny brains, as usual, flicking through the TV Channels. Anyway, I came across this documentary on Channel Four. I watched amazed as the story unfolded. It was about this young married mum who earned extra cash by taking, as far as I could tell, obscene phone calls and making bloody good money from it into the bargain. She took the calls while her kids were at school. Turned out they were talking about Premium Rate Lines. This apparently was a twenty-four hour service for guys who wanted to talk to girls about sex, fantasies and fetishes.

I thought, 'My God!'

It was just the sort of job I'd been looking for; I could look after Ma, and still get my kicks from teasing the boys. As it was a twenty-four hour service, I could look after Ma in the day time, and then when I went back to my little flat I could work most of the evening and night. I'd stay on benefits; I had to just in case I wasn't any good. Wouldn't be forever, just until I could see for myself whether or not I could make any money at it, a couple of months or so.

Next day I rang my best friend, Christine, just to confirm my thoughts and see if she agreed that it was the right way to go. Oddly enough, we both said the same. I was made for the job. I loved talking about filth at the best of times; you can ask anyone who knows me. I guess you could say it comes from working alongside the Army and RAF for eighteen years. I could swear as good as them. Tell dirty jokes as good as them. Yes, and on most occasions shag around as good as them. I loved flirting and giving blokes the come on. But for the most part I just loved messing around. It got me into trouble on many occasions, but I couldn't help myself. Prick teaser, was probably the term that readily sprang to the mind of the poor bloke I'd be chasing. I didn't mind the chasing, however it was me that did a runner when they stood their ground. I even became known to many as the Queen of double entendre. My excuse was always the same; I was brought up on Carry On films. I just loved the sauciness of it all. And that's me, in a bottle.

So, as I said earlier, all my life's experiences prepared me for the job, I'm still now to this day a 1-2-1 chat girl. Even way back when as a car-hire receptionist aged twenty-one, and separated from my first husband, whom I married at just eighteen. I guess you could say the training began. The customers who rang to book a car chatted me up over the phone and even on occasion the lads working over in the garage, used to ring me up for an obscene chat. As I look back now, though, it was all very tame, very innocent.

When I remember as to how I first started doing the calls - well, in actual fact I didn't know where to start, really. Once again my best friend, Christine, came to my rescue.

'Just phone some of the numbers. Speak to one of the girls and ask them how you go about getting a job.'

'Where would I find the numbers?' I asked her, I hadn't a clue.

'Hang on... Charlieee.' I heard her call out, her mouth away from the phone. She was shouting her son. 'He'll know,' she said back down the mouthpiece. 'He buys loads of glossy magazines. Dirty little bastard,' she added. I couldn't help chuckling to myself. I'd known Christine and her family since 1989 at RAF Benson. Her son was eight at the time, now he was a grown man of nineteen. We did the and still do get on very well, together. She's been a very good friend to me. She knew me when I was married to my RA guy. She never liked him and often told me so. Yet she neve gloated when we finally parted.

She's a shrewd lady is our Christine. She's got her ow business, now. She makes clothes for adult babies and sissie To you and me, that's grown men who like to dress up a little sissy girls or babies. Nappies, rubbers, bonnets and bib the whole damn lot! She actually started out making nightie and panty sets for larger ladies and selling them on Ebay bu she got a much better response from guys who like to dres up as babies and sissy girls. The bonus being she actually designs the clothes herself and she is able to make whateve they request, very clever is our Christine. Good luck to he is what I say. So what if we both make money from dirty bastards and their perversions.

Anyway, she gave me a couple of numbers. I rang the first one and listened to the menu options. One offered extra services so I pressed number four and was invited to join their party of sexy girls. I was instructed to leave my name and address and a contract would be sent to me by post. It was as simple as that. Well, we both waited Christine and me. Excitement and trepidation flowed through us. I hadn't got a clue, really what to expect. I just wanted to get back to work and still be able to care for Ma.

I couldn't tell Ma, though. How could I? Her poor old heart was weak enough as it was. I did try once though, a year or so later. All she said was, 'You live in a fantasy world, girl.' Little did she know I lived in everyone else's fantasy world! How could I expect her to understand, she was seventy-three for goodness sake! Something else she doesn't know, I use her first name, Edith, for one of the elderly ladies I pretend to be.

It was true, though I didn't really know what I was getting into. My ex thought me perverted because I wanted to lick cream off his naked body. As it turned out, I was mental more like for wanting to lick cream off any part of his body at all. (Yuk!) But that's another story.

The nearest I'd ever got to dirty talk was when I first arrived at Cavalry Barracks in Hounslow West back in 1979. I was being shown round the NAAFI. (Navy, Army Air Force Institute or as me Dad use to call it; No Ambition And Fuck all Interest.) This handsome young corporal came up to me and said.

"Let me get you over that till. I've always wanted to cum into money." It was the first words ever spoken to me by an Army guy. I was twenty-one and rather embarrassed. I later discovered that that's what Army guys like to do the most is embarrass young innocent girls like me. I wasn't for long though; young, innocent or embarrassed!

At last the paperwork turned up, I signed on the dotted line and returned it and waited for my Operator Manual to arrive, so the accompanying letter informed me. Three weeks later the promised manual arrived. Quite a detailed little booklet as it goes. Seemingly, we were all actresses playing a part and as such we had to have a stage name. So, I chose the name Jolene - yes after the Dolly Parton song. I wanted to be completely different, unique even. My description had to be pure fantasy also.

A, because I wasn't being the real me.

B, we were not allowed under any circumstances whatsoever to give out our personal details. The idea of this completely turned me on; I could be who ever I wanted to be. This was excellent for me, at that time, as I didn't like me much anyway. Let's face it when you lose everything you treasure most in your life it does tend to dent your self-confidence somewhat.

Firstly, I decided to be a redhead. Not strawberry blonde, but a dark red redhead with long wavy hair. I wanted to be a dress size sixteen instead of the dress size I was, twenty-two. Also, a 36 'C' cup, not the 42 'B' that I was then. To me this was the perfect size. I know I'm fat but I never wanted to be really skinny. As it turned out I was the perfect size, anyway. Just about every guy I spoke to told me so.

Unfortunately, for this one particular caller, Tom, like most men when they came through to me actually believed the description I gave. Not only didn't he like dark-haired girls of any kind he didn't like fat northern birds, either.

Which of course, I was. Obviously, you couldn't tell by my voice where I'm from originally, working along side officers on RAF camps I soon lost my northern twang. Besides, I originated from the Midlands; I did have a lot of my family up north, Yorkshire to be exact, which meant I could do northern, if I wanted. Anyway, we got chatting, I gave him my soft seductive tones, turned him on and ended up having a good giggle, as well as doing 'the business,' as I call it. Had him for thirty minutes, said he'd call again next week, which he did. Quite a few guys often did. Had him for two hours the next time, he came through for four thirty minute calls. With Premium Rate Lines that, by I.C.S.T.I.S regulation is the maximum time allowed for adult live 1-2-1 chat lines, thirty minutes at a time. Another policy of the companies is, no giving out of personal details, it is a sackable offence. Girls were not allowed to meet up with the guys, let's face it who'd want to. They could be anybody, any sick bastard. After all, some of them were!

I remember the first real nutcase I had to deal with. I'd only been doing the job a month. You got absolutely no training at all. Yes, they covered a few eventualities, topics and the like. How to steer away from unsavoury subjects they might want to talk about. How to deal with offensive callers and not to shout 'fuck off' down the phone at them, but to be polite and refined at all times. Well, all the calls are recorded and supposedly listened in to from time to time. They could listen in on your conversation at anytime and, I must admit they did do, albeit very occasionally. You had three

17

weeks to train, how and at what was never discussed. If you weren't successful they gave you another three weeks. I of course, trained in just three weeks. So, anyway this guy came through, it was his intention from the start to offend me. Any other poor bitch that could've been landed with him would have been reduced to tears. (We could hang up on a caller if we chose to, but not before telling him the reason why.) I on the other hand was made of stronger stuff. I had dealt with Army guys for several years. If you can handle them you can handle anyone. That being said, they were the best friends you could ever wish for. I stood up to them; in turn they respected and looked after me. Anyhow, back to this nutter I had on the line. He was a southerner, cockney if you like - Gangster, I thought. He asked briefly about me, I gave him my usual patter. Then he's off and running. His favourite word was the 'C' word. I'm one, he's one, everyone in the world is one. He was really bad mouthing me and everyone else, the phone line company included. My reply, laughter! What an absolute tosser! Of course, I couldn't say that, I had to be polite at all times. I just laughed and agreed. No matter what he said I laughed and agreed. He wanted to upset someone, it was obvious. However, it wasn't going to be me.

Thirty minutes he had and I had to listen to him. Well no, that's not true really, I didn't have to, but I thought at least I was preventing some other poor mare from hearing him. Besides, I've always tried to outdo the guy on the other end of the phone. You see, when I worked on Army camps that was my survival, I always tried to outdo them, by mouthing off at them, no good being nice or polite they just didn't understand that. Couldn't get it through to their addled brains. To get through to them you had to speak their language. This naturally was 'French' (swearing) I, of course am quite fluent in the language. To quite a degree, some would say!

Therefore, I'm used to the bad language these guys use, I've spoken it with finesse for many years now and still do when it's called for. So this particular caller held no surprises for me. I, on the other hand, had a few for him. So intrigued was he by my blasé attitude towards him, he called me back several times. I'd done it, I'd turned him around. I'd impressed him, you see. Now, he wanted to know the person on the other end of the phone. Perhaps it was the first time a woman had stood her ground and wasn't afraid of him.

This went on for two or three weeks. He'd phone me a couple of times a night just to chat. Yet, as it turned out, never to do the business. He got to know a bit more about me, the fantasy me, that is. And I, unfortunately, got to know a lot more about him. Talk about not wanting to meet any of the callers, this one I wouldn't meet if me Ma's life depended on it! God alone knew where he was phoning from. I think it was a club he owned, they were definitely at a bar, his mates were all around him. I could hear him talking to them sometimes. Even to them he was pretty nasty. That's what made me think he must be a gangster. One time I heard him say to one of his mates, at least, that's what he said they were.

'If you cough in my fucking face one more time, I'm going to put this cigarette out in your eye.'

I heard a low mumbled reply. 'Sorry boss. Sorry.' I couldn't help thinking, 'Good Lord! and he wonders why I wouldn't meet him!'

Oh, yes. Can you actually believe he wanted to meet me? Yeah right, I wasn't tired of living, just yet, thank you very much. So, thinking on my feet as I usually do, quite literally, this time. I went through the 'we can't give out personal details over the phone' twaddle.

Still undeterred, he continued to pursue me. He said, giving the perfect solution to our problem; 'Why don't you just copy my mobile phone number down, then can call me.' I was to say I hadn't written it down and that would cover me because the call was being recorded.

Oh yes, I could say whatever he wanted me to but like hell was I actually going to do it. Anyway I said I'd do it. Of course, I wouldn't ring and he would finally get the message. It's not that I didn't want him to ring me; I just wanted to put him off meeting me. After the first fifteen minutes of swearing he was fairly tolerable to chat with, scary, but tolerable.

I know what you are thinking, I could just as easily have hung up or refused to talk to him, but that's not me. I don't back down from anything. Besides, I was enjoying leading him a merry dance. Let's just say it was my revenge on the man. But wait, it's about to get even more complicated than that. Oh, what a tangled web we weave. He called again, this time furious that I hadn't contacted him. I reminded him that I had said I wouldn't, and had no intention of doing so.

Refusing to take no for an answer he said; 'I know you're only saying that because we're being recorded.'

Exasperated, I finally said, thinking this would completely put him off that I couldn't meet because I had difficulty getting on a train. I was in a wheelchair, I explained. I gave him a real cock and bull story and told him that the reason I did this job was to raise money to buy a prosthetic for my right leg which was severed at the knee in a car accident, that my husband was driving and that's why I was divorced now. Oh, I went into great, lengthy detail about how and when it happened. Can I spin a brilliant story when under pressure or what?! Did it put him off, though? Did it shite! On the contrary, he thought it was the best thing he'd ever heard! He wanted to meet me even more.

I know what you are all thinking, but don't forget he was one of my best callers and for every minute he was on the line, I was getting paid. Come on, boys and girls, that's what I was in it for, after all. And I loved giving him the run around. He wanted to waste his money, he could damn well waste it on me! All I knew was that he wasn't getting the better of me. Having said that, I didn't want it to be the last time he called me, either but he was really starting annoy me, now.

His reply to this information was totally unexpected. "I've got to meet you, now. We'll wait till you get your false leg; I'll send a car to pick you up. I want to take you out to a pub where no one knows us. We'll sit at a bar and I'll start an argument with you, I'll kick you really fucking hard on your leg, then I'll turn to everyone in the pub and say - fuck! She's

21

hard!" Well, I just peed myself laughing. Best of it was he was serious! In fact, the laughter which intrigued him in the beginning, actually finally put him off. He still rang from time to time, just to update me on his life. Apparently, no one understood him like I did. Oh, I understood him right enough. Thankfully, that was the end of him.

Most of the callers I did understand, or at least tried to. It had been bad enough at the beginning, I really didn't know what to say, but then over the weeks I memorised a little patter, gave my description, and then asked very seductively 'So, tell me, what's on your mind?' My voice usually did the trick. All the guys who came through commented on my voice. Initially, they would call the PRL number advertised in the Sport Newspaper or Men's Magazines and listen to a list of options. If they were new they could listen to the girls' introduction messages. Mine was: 'Hi, I'm Jolene, and I'm a fiery redhead who loves talking dirty.' We were all allocated a PIN, if the caller knew the girl he wanted to talk to he could punch in the PIN and you were straight through.

I remember this one guy I used to get quite regularly on the premium rate lines, we'd chat for a while before we did the sex chat just as we always did. However, this one particular night we were chatting away, he told me about his house and the DIY improvements he'd made to it. Then he said, "Right, I've got to go, now."

"Don't you want to cum?" I enquired, slightly put out.

"Oh, I already have," he said.

"But, I didn't get you off."

"You did that ages ago. I got off on the sound of your voice."

Blimey, now I was amazed. Or maybe it was the discussion of his DIY that really got him off!

In fact this is how Tom, the caller I mentioned earlier, came to speak to this particular redhead. Apparently he preferred blondes. Well, in reality I was half way there I was a brunette with blonde highlights. It was my voice that provoked him into choosing me. We did get on so well, he even spoke of meeting me, which of course, most of them did. He wasn't pushy or forceful. Just the polite, funny, gentleman he was. How could I meet him? I was exactly the type of girl I loathed.

I wanted to, I wanted to desperately. I really liked the sound of his voice, he seemed genuine. The sort of guy I'd been looking for all my life. We had the same sense of humour and I loved turning him on, he turned me on, too. I loved hearing him come over the phone. He got he off more than once, I can tell you! He told me all about himself. He'd had a broken marriage and a broken relationship. Same as me, really. I had two failed marriages behind me.

He made me feel good about myself and for the most part I told him a lot about me, but not everything. As much as I liked the man, I just couldn't bring myself to meet up. Not just for safety reasons, although I got my ear bent before about that from my mates Maria and Christine. But because *I* wasn't what he was looking for really, so that was that anyway.

In many ways I was living a fantasy, I was paid to be someone I wasn't. Yes, it was a great escape for me. I was living this shit life, caring for Ma in the daytime and doing dirty calls at night. Oh, the calls were all right, I enjoyed them. Where I was living, though, no one knew me. I was living in a small village, an outsider if you like. I had no friends close by, they were scattered all over the country.

Where my mother lived it was all old people. I felt as though my life had come to an end along with my mother's. The only bit of excitement I had was the dirty phone calls. So, when this wonderful sounding man came into my life, well, what else could I do? I guess that was that. I could tell the truth and risk losing him altogether. At least this way I could talk to him.

So anyway, I'd been expecting some bad calls from day one but nothing prepared me for it when it did come. I was prepared for abusive calls. You know, name calling. Slag, whore, we know where you live and all that crap. That first night I logged on to the PRL phone system, I was very apprehensive, to say the least. I didn't know what to say or expect, but after two weeks of working on the phone lines, confidence had begun to build. Finally, that long awaited dreaded caller came through. He seemed the norm to begin with; the usual wanting to lick me out and me suck his cock. Sixty-nine was the most popular topic, then and still is. Then he started to talk about things I'd never imagined, things ordinary girls should be shielded from all their lives.

So, I listened, horrified at what he was saying, what he wanted to do. I thought he was the most disgusting pervert in the world ever. Well, to be fair I didn't know many, not by then. Anyway, I just couldn't believe my ears. Me being me, I thought, right you dirty filthy bastard you want to be disgusting? Well, guess what? I can be worse than you, you fucker! And I was, I outdid him. When the thirty minutes were up, he laughed and said; "That was the best call I ever had. You're quite good at this."

My reaction to his comment was not the normal one, either, maybe because I'm not the normal chat girl. I do see every call as a challenge. Still do. I think that's what makes me the best at this job. I love getting guys to come. If I wanted to get rid and get on to the next call, I could. I became quite adept at making them shoot their load. I can't explain it, but somehow I'd feel the one in control.

Anyhow I was quite chuffed with myself, survived what I thought to be the worst call I'd ever get. When he laughed the way he did I was beginning to understand, that's what some guys like to do. They get off on being the most disgusting beast in the world ever. And believe me, he was. Turned out he was a regular to the phone service and apparently not many girls spoke to him for long. He was such a frequent user that he had a nickname. He was known as the shit piss and puke man. Oh yes, girls and boys. He wanted you to shit, piss and puke on his cock. He became one of my regulars. So, I guess you could say that was me well and truly broken in.

So, bring them on, that's what I say. Bring all the fucking dirty little wankers on!

Chapter Two

How I Became 'Jolene'

It isn't nearly as bad or depraved as it sounds; taking dirty calls for a living. On the contrary, most of the guys that come through are just your normal, everyday Joes. More often than not, they just wanted to hear a female voice at the end of a day's work. Some are lonely and hope in vain that they would meet the girl of their dreams doing chat lines.

That's what we were, you see. The girl of their dreams! They've listened to our little intros stored on the Chat Lines telephone systems to whet their appetites. We would get out of them what they were interested in and we automatically have the same interests and sexual desires. Imagination, coupled with a very arousing voice, usually did the trick. Sent them over the edge, as it were. We were their ideal girls, we made sure we were. We wanted them to come back to us time and time again and they did. Some callers really get totally hooked on the girls. I myself had one such guy, well, several really. They would ring through most nights, and as always they'd want to meet up. I'm sure some of them actually thought it was a dating line they were ringing. They'd come on line tell you all about themselves, what they looked like what they were into. Just like they were trying to match up with you. At first, we'd just exchange general info;

mine of course was completely made up. Then eventually came the sixty-four thousand dollar question, "So, where are you based?"

Which I naturally had to reply, "We are not allowed to give out that information."

"How are we supposed to meet?" would come the blundering reply.

"We're not permitted to 'meet' our callers. This is a chat line not a date line." Of course by now, the penny's dropped, "" Brrrrr... Amazingly the line's goes dead.

For the most part, that's what it is all about, really. They truly believe we are like the girls they see in the magazines and papers. However, not all of them are easily fooled. I've been accused several times of doing my ironing or housework and that they bet I was some dirty old granny sat in my rollers getting kicks out of talking to young blokes! Bless 'em!

Surprisingly, what maybe some people wouldn't believe is that a large percentage of the calls are from guys coming on just to chat. We do two types of calls. Well, two mainly. The calls come through under several different headings. We are asked to record several different messages under many different guises. There are the soft chat lines found under 0906 and the adult sex chat lines 0909. However, if they come through as soft chat we are not allowed to start the dirty talk first. The guys themselves have to instigate the adult hard chat. This is funnily frustrating for some of the guys who don't know the difference. A few guys obviously don't know what to say, yes I know you'd think all guys were the same and know what they are after. A lot are eighteen year olds and have never even seen a pussy let alone know what to talk about. So, they dial the number, some listen and select the first girl on the carousel, that's a carousel of recorded messages. If you were first on the carousel that time you'd get the first idiot of the night!

You could hear the desperation in their small, shy voices. They so wanted to hear you talk about 'sex' and say all the naughty swear words. Of course when you didn't, they usually swore and then hang up. Naturally, you'd get underage lads trying to do a call with you. You were told to ask the year they were born. If that didn't work which of course it didn't always, you, the chat girl would ask them what they wanted. They would use childlike words to talk about your private parts, their words. Once I asked this one lad what he did at school, after he told me I laughed and hung up. Even back then I was a wicked bitch! So, eventually either in frustration or embarrassment they'd hang up within the minute. Or I'd just tell them point blank, "I'm sorry, but I don't believe you're eighteen." Mind you I sometimes did this even if I did think they were old enough, just for devilment! Then I'd have to end the call. But sometimes it was quite humorous hearing them struggle to use the adult terminology for dirty talk.

The 0909 numbers were completely different you could straight away get on with the filthy talk, well, it was expected. So, after giving it some consideration I came up with a scenario and I decided to tell my callers that I was a part-time still life model at the local art college. I became very good at deception. I told them my biggest fantasy was at the night school itself and how I lay completely naked, staring at the young eighteen year old students and mature students, naturally. Watching them blush with embarrassment and how they would quickly turn their gaze away only to be drawn back to my naked form again and how sometimes I would have to change my position on the chaise longue and give those naughty young students a flash of my little shaven haven. Then, continuing with the erotic fantasy, I'd tell the caller how I imagined they'd all come over to me, take out their erections and proceed to masturbate over me. How I would moan, writhing about sliding my fingers into my wet pussy. Well, as you can imagine, this brought them off every time! Of course, sometimes the same caller came back so I'd have to think of a different fantasy. Also, by then I'd have some idea about what he liked to talk about. And, if it was really good and had him cuming in minutes, I'd use it on the next caller that came through. Jolene gradually became the new woman in my life and she made me the woman I am today.

Over the weeks Jolene developed and gradually I gained experience in the art of getting men off. Oh, don't get me wrong, it sometimes is a two way street. I actually had my first multiple orgasms over the phone. It was totally wild, the combination of the guy's sexy, husky voice and him saying what he wanted to do to me, wow! I didn't think I'd ever stop cuming. The odd thing was the fantasy. It was an adult baby fantasy. Something I'd never heard of nor had I done before. I remember he had this soft, well spoken voice, I love posh blokes and he had a voice which seemed to penetrate my brain, very sexy voice he had, spell-binding almost. He told me his fantasy - him baby, me mother. I had to say I'd put a nappy on him and wash him around his cock and arse. Dry him then put powder or cream on him. Oh, I had to go into great detail. Finally, I would lift him on to my knee and breastfeed him whilst stroking his cock through the nappy. Then he'd tell me he wanted me to cream for him. Baby was hungry so I had to produce cream for him. He'd tell me he'd climb off my knee and nestle between my legs and then proceeded to tell me how good I smelt and how sweet I tasted and how he loved rubbing his face between my hairy pussy lips. The strange thing is you get so easily lost in the words, the way they are spoken. It's mesmerising. You get caught up in the moment and can easily understand how it affects them, too. You can hear the excitement the caller is feeling as I'm certain they do at their end. It was so wild, so different. Not because the bloke was wearing a nappy, or it was a mother and son incestuous thing. It was his words of encouragement saying. "Come on, cream for baby, cream for me." What with his words, the sound of his heavy breathing and him wanking, the whole build up to it. I was so turned on I just couldn't stop cuming. Bear in mind, I'd done several calls prior to this so I was well turned on anyway.

I had him quite a few times over the weeks and the fantasy in reality became really heightened. I can say, in all honesty, I always had great sex with him!

What sort of sex had I experienced prior to these calls, you must be wondering? Well, I had lots of sex but somehow or other not much experience. Even though I'd had two husbands and several fiancés, yet still I'd not got a clue as to what men and sex were all about.

I think that's what I like most about the calls is the diversity of them. Don't get me wrong, I don't like them all. Let me ask you, do you like every part of your job? Nobody does, I put it down to the same principle. I don't like every call, but thankfully, they don't very last long. And, if I'm really lucky, they don't come back.

Sometimes though, I think that's what some of them want, for you not to like them. I think they actually get some sort of kick out of it. Some of them come back time and time again. I know what I'm saying; I've put it to the test. I've pretended I like them and you don't hear from them again. Let them think for one minute you're revolted by them and they just keep coming back.

That being said it's not true in all cases, a few are just really sick bastards!

That very first night I did the lines, I was terrified to say the least. What of, I don't know. They didn't know me from Adam. It's not as though they could track me down, or stalk me or anything. I think, as with most things, it was just fear of the unknown. Anyway, it wasn't that bad, some didn't last for very long, and a couple of minutes was all it took. Still does, for some. Yes, I am that good. My record, one minute twenty-five seconds. And, I don't mean occasionally, I mean quite a few times. Some of them, every time they come through, never seem to go for very long.

However, that first night, I could only stay logged on for an hour and a half. You could log on and off for as long as you liked just as long as you remembered to log off otherwise the phone system would just keep putting the calls through. I didn't log off because it was bad, it wasn't. The guys were quite complimentary for the most part. I was really very nervous, that's all. Deep down, you see, I'm still that shy timid girl of my childhood. Once I'd built up a bit of confidence, however, I would soon be off and running, as always. What did surprise me most of all, which quite shocked me actually, was how wet I was. I'd gone to the loo shortly after I'd logged off only to find my pussy was absolutely soaking wet. My panties were saturated. I had no idea how turned on I'd been. I'd been so worked up about doing the calls; I hadn't even noticed the effect it had had on me. Turned out to be quite a bonus, however, guys love to hear you play with your pussy over the phone and mine being so damn wet was an absolute bonus, it used to drive them wild. Of course, like me, it was all an act, most of the time. Listening to the vibrator buzzing away and me moaning took them right over the edge. Naturally, to be able to hear me moan and the vibrator at the same either meant I was a contortionist or a bloody good actress!

"Ooh, can you hear that?" I'd ask sounding all breathless. So they should hear it, it was resting against the mouth piece of my phone!

A great deal of it was boring to say the least, the quick call, a short toss and they'd be gone, then the next one came through and he'd be the same, sucking them off was all they wanted to talk about. These calls do sometimes grate after a while. But then, a great sounding guy would come through. One with a bit of chat, or a really adventurous mind. Or even like my man, Tom, a great sense of humour. Many times he accused me of been a laughter line. But thankfully, that didn't put him off.

That was four years ago, now and we are still together. We met at my place just two weeks after his initial phone call and three weeks before he went away on holiday. We got on so well together, we've hardly been apart since. Even though he lived in Kent and me in Nottinghamshire, I came for a visit the day he came back off holiday and hardly ever went back. I kept my flat on for a year, just in case. Now, I've permanently moved in. My dog, Sasha, the two cats and me. I know it was a big risk meeting a stranger, someone I'd only spoken to over the telephone. I certainly wouldn't have wanted one of my friends to do it, I can tell you and, boy oh boy, did I get a load of stick from all my friends. But they hadn't spoken to him. He had told me so much about himself, real personal stuff and I told him all about my life, too. Plus; and it's a big plus, I own a Rottweiller. Yes, Sasha is a rottie. Worships Tom, now and he her. Not bad for a bloke who doesn't like dogs and detests cats, by the way. Even when I go back to see Ma now and again, she stays with him; and they say dogs are a good judge of character. Well, she's definitely right about this one.

I continued working for the premium rate lines for a year after I moved in with Tom, but unfortunately the calls started to dry up. I still wanted to work so I decided to look for other PRL Companies to sign up with so I surfed the internet for them. However, I came across websites for Call Back companies. How call-backs works is, instead of guys paying for the calls via BT, they actually paid by credit or debit cards sometimes even cheques and postal orders. In addition, instead of them just calling a premium rate number, it's usually a regular landline number to call or like myself I use an 0870 number which goes over the top of my landline number. The caller gives their details over the phone and actually books a call with one of the chat girls. Anyway, the website said they were looking for recruits and interested parties could apply on their website, which I did.

They contacted me by phone two days later, gave me a trial, and then they started me on taking the calls.

What amazed me the most, in the beginning was that I had to be different ages, sizes and hair colour for any given caller, whatever their request. Well, it was a fantasy line after all, and we had to be whatever it took to fulfil their fantasies. However, what truly blew my mind was that I had to be several different girls to the same man! I mean, for goodness sakes, how could they not know? For the PRLs all I ever was, was Jolene.

So, no matter what, whatever it took, I did it. I even managed to change my voice slightly after a bit of practice. Thankfully, I could do posh, common (because I am), young and old. The old bit came easy because I was actually in my late forties, at that time.

On the whole, though, the job is like no other. A great deal of the guys who come through are gentlemen, polite but just a bit perverted, that's all! They always thank you after we've finished the chat, some say I'll speak to you again and most often times, they do. They are normal guys who just want to get away from the norm and be a bit abnormal, shall we say. For the most part it is what it is, fantasy. There's definitely a skill to it. There are key words to listen for. A particular phrase that flicks their switch. I do love the fact that if I choose to I can get them off with just a few chosen words. For the most part men are dirty bastards, the dirtier the fantasy, the better. More often than not it's something they wouldn't dream of doing with their partner.

A. because it's too disgusting or degrading to their partner.

B. it would be unthinkable that their partner would want them to do what they were talking about, anyway. They just have these wild thoughts running around their brain and the only way to stop this is to ring me, and others like me.

The main reasons for these pent up feelings that guys harbour, comes from lack of communication on their part. Some guys take themselves and their sexual desires far too

36

seriously. Maybe if we girls weren't such prudes, sometimes, and were a bit more adventurous ourselves we could enjoy their fantasies, too. Of course if the guys weren't so damn scared of their own fantasies, then they wouldn't maybe feel the need for girls like me. A lot of them are quite tame fantasies, like sniffing panties or wanking into them or even wearing them. There's nothing wrong with a bit of kinkiness in your life. Spices it up! You know, variety and all that.

Anyway, at first, all went well working for the Call Back Company. Earned some good money, spoke to some strange and interesting guys. It was completely different to PRLs where you could log on and off the phone system of PRLs as you pleased; with Call Backs you could stay available to take calls day and night. In addition, the calls had a minimum time span, ten minutes to a landline and five minutes to a mobile. Whereas the guys coming through the phone system would just simply hang up when they'd had enough. The biggest bonus was the fact that you could take fewer calls for more money. All the time you are logged on to the PRLs you constantly receive calls, at eighteen pence a minute you had to do a hell of a lot of chat to earn good money.

Where you'd take maybe a hundred calls through the PRLs in the course of several hours to earn fifty pounds, with the Call Backs I could earn the same fifty pounds from twenty-five calls spread over the day. This way you weren't tied to the phone with constant calls for five or six hours.

As I said, all went well to begin with but unfortunately the woman who owned the company thought she owned the girls, too. She expected a lot more than I was prepared to give, she expected you to be available to take calls 24/7. Every time I wanted time off she gave me the third degree, so I looked for another Call Back company, this time I searched the classified ads in the adult sporty newspapers sold on a Sunday, this is where you can find the biggest selection of Call Back Companies.

I can't honestly say why I chose the Call Back Company I did, I can only say I'm very glad I did. It's thanks mainly to the lady who owned that particular company that I had the confidence to start out on my own and also she advised me every step of the way. I did very much enjoy working with her, but why earn £1.50 for a ten-minute landline call when I could earn £12 for the same call, working for myself.

This was the beginning of my journey. My journey through the lust and lives of the many men who use Call Backs on a regular basis. Except, this is a call back of a different kind. You see, I am the receptionist, all the girls the guys talk to and of course the owner of the newest and best call back company running today.

Therefore, readers, enjoy the rest of the journey. A journey of unimaginable fantasies stored inside the minds of many men who use the callbacks. A journey through the following pages in the hope of better understanding of what makes our men's minds tick, and why they desperately feel the need to voice their deepest, darkest desires.

Chapter Three

From Sixteen To Seventy-Three

This is not just about the age ranges I cover, it's about the small minority of callers who talk to girls and ladies aged from sixteen to seventy-three. Most guys, who come on line, will either speak to a sixteen year old or a seventy-three years old. Some like to fantasise about innocent young schoolgirls while others like to fantasise about mature, experienced ladies.

Each fantasy has a specific requirement. Sixteen years olds are, for the main part, young, sweet tasting school girls, and are small breasted with smooth pussies. However, occasionally, they like to think their particular schoolgirl has big boobs. Usually these girls are, in their minds, young innocent things who need to be taken care of by big strong, worldly men who know what to do to please their women. In fact, in reality, the opposite is true. They haven't got a clue how to please a woman in bed or more likely, are just too lazy to please a woman sexually. Quite often they feel threatened by a real woman. Young girls have no experience, therefore, they have no expectations. And, of course, for some, it's simply because they are inadequately endowed.

Most often with schoolgirl fantasies, it is the idea of a dirty little schoolgirl who makes the grown up man's cock hard. In other words, the dirty old bastard's cock hard!

Here's a short, yet very common example. I get this one guy come through like so many others, on a regular basis. Everything I say to him he replies to very breathily and is obviously very turned on. "You dirty little bitch!" Or, if I want to do to him everything he asks of me, again he'll say. "You fucking dirty little bitch!" Then shoot his load.

This, for most schoolgirl fantasists, is the turn on; the sixteen year old is so unbelievably very dirty.

Just about all guys talk about things they can never hope to have. It's beyond the realms of possibility and that's the reason why they talk about it. Because they can't do it for whatever reason, makes them want it more and more until the obsession becomes so strong they need some sort of release to get it out of their systems.

Needless to say, the opposite is true at the other end of the age range, seventy-three. It's because they desire a dirty old bitch with an extremely hairy pussy and well used pussy lips with big saggy boobs, who's going to give them a fucking good dirty time, and of course they have years of experience behind them. In the mind of the caller, she might be an old dear who loves talking dirty because, after all, there is something quite kinky about a refined, mature woman who loves getting men off. So therefore she must be a real dirty old bitch! As you know by now, guys do love it dirty. Believe me; these guys really do know how to please a woman in bed.

These guys are totally perverse and will talk about anything under the sun that's extreme. Why? Actually, it's usually because they're simply fed up with their boring mundane sex lives. They feel the need to be as disgusting and perverse as they can be to satisfy a deep animal lust that they are unable to fulfil in real life.

However, the callers who like to talk to both ends of the age range; these are the dirtiest ones of all. Not only do they see themselves as the corrupters of young innocent minds and want to violate young virginal bodies, they also want to shag her dirty old granny in the next room. I hate to say it, but these are usually the most interesting calls that I do, because they are so open minded and perverted that literally, anything goes. You are allowed to be as dirty and disgusting as a woman can be without actually having to do anything! Believe me, for some reason it is so liberating and it feels quite cleansing, as I'm sure it must be to the caller. Quite often at the end of a particular dirty obscene call, the guy will say, "Phew, I needed to get that out my system. I feel better, now. I can get on with things." And basically, I truly believe that is what these phone calls are all about. Relieving pent up sexual feelings they can't get rid of anywhere else.

It's an odd thing what turns a man on, especially when it comes to the age of a woman. I have this one regular who comes through fairly often, two or three times a week. He started off by having Elle, one of my sixteen year olds. I don't know why, but I always refer to the girls I'm pretending to be, as my girls or one of my girls. Even when I tell Tom, now my partner (not in the business) about a caller and the girl he's spoken to, I always say, she said this or she did that. It's strange that I separate myself from the women I'm pretending to be. It just comes so naturally to me. I suppose it's because I feel as though I'm someone else when I'm doing the call.

Anyway, we have a good twenty minute chat as always, me the naughty, cheeky schoolgirl who turns on the dirty old man. Nothing kinky, just the usual, oral, anal and shagging fantasy. This went on for several months. By the way, he's even had me as Dee, the receptionist a few times. Allegedly, she's forty-eight. At least, that's the age I say she is. Then one day he came through and asked who was the oldest lady I had on. I informed him of Mable, gave her description and her age, seventy-three and he said he'd give her a go.

I usually give them the name, age and description of women friends I actually know. Some of my most popular girls are my best friends. If she's a brunette, it's my friend, Christine. She's chunky in real life, so if they want a big girl, I use her for that, too. If they want a small petite woman I use my friend, Marie. She's got mousy brown hair with blonde streaks. For the busty, bubbly blonde it's Rosie. For the mature, curvy lady it's my friend Yvonne. Yes, they all know I use them. There are only three people who don't know I use their names and descriptions, but who probably will do by the time they get their hands on this book! They are my friend Val, my auntie Pam and my mother, Edith. If I don't use these ladies exactly, I use a variation of them. It's not very often I use myself, only very occasionally. However, I do try to become the friend I'm describing when I do the call, helps me better to get into character. Although, I sometimes give different names to represent the different friends I use. They also cover every age group in the late twenties upwards. The only ones I completely invent are the sixteen year olds. I try to be as sweet and innocent as I can be and somewhat naive, of course.

I love it when a caller ask if I've got genuine sixteen year olds working for me. Yes, of course, I tell them.

"Only, I went to this other company," this one caller said, "and she sounded more like a forty-six!" I had to chuckle, I knew which company he was talking about; I used to work for them myself. I even did a two girl call with one of her ladies, she didn't sound much like a sixteen year old even to me either. She was supposed to be eighteen, that particular time. Never in a million years!

Obviously I never said anything to the caller. All I said was (which is what I always say to the question), "Well, they tell me they're sixteen."

But the biggest thrill of all is when they ring the office back and tell me she was the best sixteen year old they've ever spoken to. I think to myself, I know I was!

The biggest kick of all, though, is when *I* do a two girl call. Thankfully, I've only ever had to be a sixteen year old and a forty year old. Not the same age. I even argued with myself and called myself names to the caller.

Tom has heard me and has absolutely wet himself.

"You are good, it's got to be said." He's even made me try it out on his friends and family, they are always astounded. He's always so amazed, bless him. He says, after I've spoken to one of his mates, "And, they even know you're doing it!" Well, what can I say, when you're good, you're good. But there again, he knows I'm good because he's had me. I suppose that's why he's always supported me on this venture.

Anyway getting back to this caller I'm telling you about, who's trying out Mable for the first time. As usual, I put on the oldest, croakiest sounding voice I could do, she's supposed to be in her seventies, after all. I always call the guy 'dearie' and 'mmmm' a lot and take a bit of time over my reply, well; I'm not quite so quick to respond nowadays. I also remember that my late friend Mable used to be a servant girl when she was very young, so I sometimes used this as my opening chat. How I used to be courted by the master's young son and how I couldn't refuse his attentions or I'd be sacked and out on my ear. Of course, referring to; 'in my young day', quite a lot helped somewhat. It all added to the authenticity of the elderly chat. So, of course, the caller was hooked into the fantasy, and naturally, he wanted it as dirty as possible. Oooh, and believe me it was dirty. What men find horny about a wrinkled old arsehole that turns them on so, I've got no idea. But, by God it does, and how. It sends them into a sexual frenzy!

Of course, it goes without saying, he absolutely loved Mable and now he has her all the time. And yet, he still doesn't know it's all the same person. This, in its way, is quite amazing. Think about it. He speaks to me as Dee, the receptionist. Then to Elle for a call, then back to me to book a call with Mable. After Mable herself, back to me. So, in the space of about an hour, he has spoken to me four times as three different women. Me, twice as Dee and then Elle and Mable. And, don't forget, he's also done several calls with Dee.

I honestly think that's why I can fool so many guys, I actually take on the persona of the woman I'm pretending to be. Don't get me wrong, I don't fool all the guys all the time, some have found me out. They've been so amazed by my diversity they've gone along with the fantasy of me being whoever they want me to be for that particular call.

One regular of mine sussed me out after a few calls, but didn't let on. I didn't realise he knew until several calls later when he asked me if I fancied being a schoolgirl for a change. I stuttered, surprised and asked what he meant. He said quite matter of factly, could I do a schoolgirl fantasy with him. He'd always had me as a pensioner prior to this. I chuckled for a moment or two and asked him outright if he was aware I did all the calls. Oh, yes. He knew, he assured me, knew it from the third call.

"And, you don't mind?" I queried.

"Not in the least. Why should I, I get what I want out of the call and I can say without a doubt it's the best call back I've ever used. I nearly always have different girls with other companies because I don't like having the same girls. With you, however, I can still get whatever fantasy I want and I know it'll be the best call back I will ever get."

I know this to be true because we've been doing the chat now for well over a year. I have to say we do some extremely horny fantasies. He's got a very sexy, intimate voice and it really is just like it's the two of us.

When he comes through to book a call he tells me the fantasy he wants to do. Sometimes I'm Mable, seventy-three who's a very worried pensioner querying the reduction of her pension. She's obviously willing to do anything to get her money increased, again! So, of course I start by ringing his office, which, in reality, is his home land line. I'm distressed by the fact my pension has dropped down considerably and I can no longer afford to pay my rent. After pleading with him and all but selling myself to him he asks if I mind if he gets his cock out.

"Your cock?" I ask, sounding surprised. "Why young man, I haven't had a bit of cock for such a long time, I've almost forgot what one looks like."

To which he replies, "Well, if you like, I could come round and refresh your memory. Do you like sucking cock?"

"Mmmm, I could suck on that big fat fucker of yours for hours!"

"Oooh, you dirty old bitch. I'm coming round right now."

And that's how the fantasy would begin.

I just hope when I'm really in my seventies I can still turn a man on the way Mable does. She seems to be every caller's favourite old bird!

With the schoolgirl fantasy, he is the truant officer ringing to see why I wasn't at school. Again, the problem could be sorted with sexual favours. I quite enjoy our little scenarios. I have told him it's just me, because we do actually chat from time to time and I've told him I do all the calls. I asked him did he mind. He told me he had a good time on the phone with me and that's all that mattered. He is without a doubt an absolute gentleman and he does have such a lovely sounding voice. It gives me great pleasure to do him.

I always tell my partner, Tom, about all the calls I do, and he always agrees with all my men. They come to me time and time again because I'm very good at what I do, and if it's a new guy he always asks, "Another satisfied customer?"

"Yep" I reply.

"He'll be back, then." He smiles his smile of pride, happy to be proud of his girl.

Don't get me wrong, I don't satisfy every guy who comes through for a call. Some come through and hang up before the time's up and I never hear from them again, for whatever reason there's a lot of guys like this. Some ring to make enquiries and never book a call with me. For all I know some don't come back after two or three calls because they have sussed me out and are not interested anymore.

Of course, we do get a lot of guys who are what we call, floaters, they are not loyal to any one Call Back Company. Many guys just lose their bottle, terrified of being found out. Or it's just curiosity and they decide it wasn't what they were looking for after all. However, the guys I do get always praise me for the service me and my girls give them.

For some other guys who've sussed me out, it's taken them quite some time. A certain regular of mine who comes through three or four times a night, not every night, he usually calls every two or three weeks, always books a ten minute call to his mobile at the cost of sixteen pounds a call. That's some money he spends!

Every time he comes on, he always asks the same thing. "Who's the dirtiest woman you've got on line, tonight?" Usually, the woman has to be in her forties or fifties, preferably married. It's always with a different woman. Doesn't matter who he has just as long as she's a real dirty old bitch.

I've often said to Tom, "For goodness sakes how many different ways can a dirty old bitch be dirty?" That being said he never sussed for a hell of a long time. It was only one time when he thought I sounded like the woman on reception did he become suspicious, but even then he wasn't really certain. It was my own fault really, I got a bit chatty one night. I'd taken a few hours off, put the phone on answer machine. "Sorry, all our girls are busy at present. Please try later." Yeah, right, I'm out stuffing my fat face!

Every time I take some time off, this is what I have do. If, however, I'm away from the phone for a few days I don't place any ads in the paper the weekend before and the message informs the caller that; "Due to unforeseen circumstance the office is closed for forty-eight hours." Yes, it's a great job but it is a tie. I've had no real time off for three years. I'm not complaining, it's just that every now and again you have to take a break from the ringing of the bloody phone. Don't forget I am 24/7.

This particular night we decided to go out for a meal and I'd had a bit to drink. Well, it had been a bit of a quiet day so, occasionally, I take the evening off. Not too long after I'd got back in, the phone went; it was my regular looking for the dirtiest bitch I'd got on line. As I said I'd been out for a meal I was a bit tiddly and we started chatting. He was a Geordie, I love Geordies, and I lived that up way for fifteen years. I was a little nostalgic. We had quite a chuckle.

Even so, it wasn't that night he sussed me because I did him as Dee the receptionist. It was the next time he came through he started to query who I was. So, I told him, I don't know why, I just did. He was absolutely blown away. Could not believe every woman he'd ever spoken to was me. Oh well, I thought. I've just lost myself one of my best callers.

I think the reason I told him was I couldn't lie to him so openly. His reply blew me away.

"You are so good. I totally didn't have a clue. You even changed personalities. They were some of the best calls I've ever had."

"So you really don't mind?" I ventured to ask.

"No, not in the least." And he's proved it by coming back to me time and time, again. He would still tell me the fantasy he wanted, the age I had to be and whether or not I was married. He's a really nice lad and I'm glad I told him. But he, like all the rest doesn't know the real me. That's just for one man in my life, my Tom.

But, what really blows everyone away, myself included, is the two-girl calls I do. They don't come through that often, but when they do, again, there's only me to do them. I remember the owner of the last company I worked for telling me of another girl who did the two-girl calls, very successfully, by all accounts. But I wasn't sure. I practiced a few times on friends of mine and Tom's and of course, Tom himself. Finally, everyone convinced me to do it. Lo and behold, not long after I get my first go at a paying customer. Thankfully, he wanted a sixteen year old and a woman in her forties. I hate to say it but it was a doddle! At one point I was arguing with myself and slagging myself off! I actually think it works better with just one girl because you don't talk over each other and end up having to repeat everything. Even so, twenty-four quid for a ten minute chat, sometimes they don't even last that long. It's money for old rope. That's another reason why they are so few and far between, too expensive. Two girls is twice the cost, naturally!

I had a guy through just the other day wanting a two girl call. He wanted me to use a vibrator on the 'other' girl. So, in between making slurping noises I had to encourage her to use the vibrator good and hard.

"Go on, you dirty bitch, lick my hairy pussy." I said in a slightly deeper voice. Followed by, "Mmmm, yeah, ooh, you taste so good!" in a slightly higher softer voice. The older me would do all the commentating.

"Can you hear that filthy whore moaning in between my wet pussy lips." Of course he couldn't care less by now what he could hear, the thought of two women going at each other hammer and tongue and the two different sounding voices was enough to convince him and send him over the edge. For some strange reason they never seem to last long.

How good am I at convincing them I'm a sixteen year old? I'll give you some idea; I have a couple of callers who give tips or gifts of money to my teenage schoolgirls when they call them. A few guys have actually rung back and said the girl they spoke to was underage, couldn't have been more than thirteen, he informed me. One guy who used Elle, quite often gave 'her'a ten pound tip. One particular time she was so good, she got fifty quids' worth of tips in just one day. I sound silly and a bit dim or fluff - my words. It all adds to the fantasy of me being just sixteen years old.

When I'm asked how come I have so many sixteen year olds working for me, I tell them that's easy, I pay better than the other companies. Well, I do I keep all the money myself! Yes, you might think I'm conning them and yes, in a way, I am. But they still get the best call they've ever had. You put me against a real teenager and I know which one they'll come back to.

The vast majority of the guys that use this service on a regular basis already know they are not speaking to a sixteen year old. Again, I remember the woman I once worked for before telling me she had a genuine eighteen year old working for her. I could hear her rubbing her hands over the phone she was so chuffed. It all fell through though not long after. She just hadn't the experience to get a guy off or to be as dirty as the men think an eighteen year old should be. They would use her two or three times and then never ask for her again.

It's all just a fantasy, like all the calls we do. It's not about conning anybody. It's about, , giving the guy the best call I can, for me anyway. And, I know they've had the best call because it's me they are doing the call with. Maybe this is the main reason I've never employed anyone else. Plus the fact they could be better than me, God forbid!

Chapter Four

The Things I've Been

Once upon a time I lived a very simple life. I worked hard from the age of fourteen. First, I worked in a factory, then in a shop and in a pub. Not long after this, I became a NAFFI girl on Army bases. On these, I worked as a cleaner, a mess hand, then eventually was promoted to a Steward II working on RAF bases. So, you could say I've been a shop assistant, a barmaid, pot washer and a silver service waitress.

However, what I never expected to be when I grew up was a transvestite, a transsexual or a she-male. I've been a dominatrix, a torturer and a dirty old whore. And most bizarrely; a dog handler! The one thing I never expected to be was one of the best chat girls for getting men off over the phone.

"So, what do you do for a living?" my hairdresser asks, expecting the usual chit chat. What she didn't expect was to be shocked to her roots. Well, she was doing mine at the same time!

"Well, I make men cum over the phone!" What a head turner that statement is. Oh, yes, I've told my hairdresser what I do for a living. She, her girls and the customers lapped it up. In fact, for the most part, just about everyone I've told has lapped it up. They all wanted to know the same thing, what do they or I talk about. Even my bank manager in my home town of Newley wanted to know what I talked about.

I couldn't tell them the really bad ones, of course. They, like a lot of people just wouldn't understand. I mean, I didn't understand, not at first. It's all talk really, nothing more. Yes, they are dirty like you wouldn't believe, some quite perverse. I'm a firm believer in the saying; 'Those who talk about don't do it' and they don't. Well, I'm ninety percent sure!

The calls I did feel able to talk about had everyone I told in fits of laughter. I suppose that's why I decided to put pen to paper. Some of it, I must say, sounds so farfetched and contrived to be easily believed. But believe me it doesn't matter how warped your mind was you couldn't make half this stuff up!

However, one of my favourite calls I could tell them about was this one particular night I was logged on to the PRLs a woman's voice came over the phone... She asked, slightly het up, "Do you like having your pussy licked?"

To which I replied, "Of course. Doesn't every woman? I settled myself down into what I thought to be a lesbian chat. (Yes, we get those, too.)

"Here then," she snorted out an unexpected reply. "You tell my husband." She'd actually handed him the phone because I heard a sulky mumbled,

"Hello?"

Smirking to myself, I asked, "Don't you like licking pussy, then?" The sound of the receiver being hung up was my only reply.

Chuckling to myself, I thought, the poor bastard, but I didn't really know who I felt more sorry for, him or her.

These are the softer calls, the funny ones, and ones that are repeatable in certain company, a bit like the next caller.

This one guy I spoke to regularly on call backs, was actually caught in the act while we were doing the chat. His particular fetish was sniffing used panties and talking about licking pussy and dirty knickers and their different smells. He even told me about all the massage parlours he visited every other week. He would spend the whole hour just licking the girl's pussy. In turn, she sucked him off. Most times he would bring back a pair of their panties as souvenirs. Anyway, he would phone me two or three times a week. He'd always be in the same place, in the flat of his wife's best friend. Which I found a bit odd and said as much to him after our umpteenth chat.

I was interested in silly things like how could he access her flat so often? At first, I thought he mustn't be married because of his obsession with other girls' pussies. God! His face and teeth must stink, if not he must be the best scrubbed man in the world and have the cleanest teeth. It must cost his wife a small fortune in mouth rinse.

So anyway, over a period of time I discovered that he was married and the flat he used did indeed belong to the best friend of his wife. So how did he manage to access her flat so freely, Apparently he'd done some building work there because he was an actual builder and had her front door key cut on the quiet!

Aren't some of them cheeky fucking bastards? Even me with all my experience and knowledge can't believe what they get up to sometimes.

Then this one time we are doing the call, I heard him whisper down the phone.

"I can hear something..."

No more was said, and then I can hear voices, his and someone else's. A couple of minutes later I hear him saying. "I've got to go, now. I've been found out."

Well, I flew down the stairs, Tom was sat outside drinking lager, awaiting my return.

"You'll never guess what!" I burst out on to the patio. "He's been caught red-handed; the Smelly Knickers man!" I explained.

"No!" he gasped, amazed. He knew all about the caller and his fetish. So, when I told him he'd been caught wearing this girl's knickers on his face, his cock in one hand and his mobile phone in the other, we absolutely pissed ourselves. Needless to say, he's never been back since.

Can you imagine it, though? We've often discussed it, Tom and I. Coming back home to the safety of your flat, and then creeping up the stairs to the sound of someone in your bedroom. Then, opening the door to find your best friend's hubby laid there with his hard cock in his hand and your favourite knickers on his head. I mean, what's a girl to say!? 'Can't wait to tell your missus!' springs to mind, amongst a barrage of obscenities. Still, I've always said it takes all kinds to make a world. Any how! Wouldn't you've just loved to have known how he explained that one away!

Some of my close friends say if it's on their minds, they must want to do it. Well, for some fantasies, that's true. A lot of them though, either haven't the balls, the opportunity or the inclination to carry them out. Ask yourself what sort of girl would comply with half the usual perversions that men wish to bestow on us let alone the really outlandish ones!

I remember a couple of times I had one of my close friends with me on a visit when I did the premium rate line calls. They themselves were curious as to what was said. One friend even listened in over my mobile phone while I spoke to a caller on my landline. She was utterly gob smacked; she said she didn't realise people spoke like that. The thing is; guys like to hear women swear like common trollops, especially in bed or during sex. They want us to be demure and ladylike out of bed, but in bed we're expected to behave like whores.

Mind you, the cheek of some people I've let into the secret of what I do for a living! And as luck would have it, I actually had one of my mates with me at this particular time because otherwise no one would have believed it!

My friend, Marie and I were sat chatting in my flat one afternoon, when the phone rang; I wasn't logged on to the phone system at that time because I only worked at night.

Anyhow, I picked up the receiver and a man's voice asked if I was Ms Jennifer Ainslie-Turner, which I affirmed to be correct. Turned out he was from a credit card company ringing to confirm my details then congratulated me on the acceptance of my application. Of course, he'd asked me what I did for a living, he didn't query my reply just carried on with his line of questioning. Ten minutes later the call ended with my expected credit card on its way.

Two hours later, my friend and I were still chatting, when I started receiving texts on my mobile. I read them, they were very cryptic to say the least. At first I thought it was my best friend Christine, well, it was something she was apt to do. The texts were nothing much, not to begin with. Just the usual, 'Hi' followed by, 'what you doing?' Then it asked, 'have you guessed who it is yet?' Anyway, by this time I was getting so pissed off that I eventually refused to reply to another text unless they said who they were. It only turned out to be the guy who'd been questioning me about my credit card application. The fucking cheeky bastard, he only wanted some freebie dirty phone calls. I teased with a couple of dirty texts, and then left him high and dry. Told him if he wanted to do a dirty phone call, he could ring the premium rate lines in the paper.

I had the same sort of thing when I first started staying with Tom. Again, while I was working on the PRLs. This time it was a BT engineer. I'd rung him because our phone lines were down, he tested the lines, said the fault was at our junction box and would send out an engineer three days later. Of course, I had to inform him of my dilemma and he helped by forwarding all my landline calls to my mobile. Then he started with sending texts wanting freebies, soon told him where to go and what number to ring.

Quite right, too, Tom said. I'm the only one who gets it for free! I've been many things in my time but I'm no mug especially when it comes to giving away my time and talent.

A talent? I hear you asking yourselves. A talent for getting men off over the phone! Well, there is more to it than heavy breathing and moaning down the phone. I mean, I've actually convinced some of my callers that not only am I a different age, hair colour or size, I've convinced them I'm a different sex! Yes, to a small minority of callers I've been a transvestite, a transsexual and a she-male. Now, you must agree, that takes a certain kind of talent.

That's the one thing I've learnt from the other companies, we can be whatever the caller wants us to be. But how on earth do you pretend to be a guy?! Well, it's no easy task, I can tell you. I have got a bit of a rough sounding voice when I want it to be and I can swear like a bloke. The domination I've done makes you come across as being quite assertive. The rest I make up as I go along. It is what I'm good at after all, make-believe. The names I gave were either Simone or Pauline. I think that speaks for itself. Simone I usually used for the domination calls as well as Pamela and Christine. They are always deep and gruff sounding, too. All adds to the ambiance.

59

Anyway, the first 'guy' I had to be was the transvestite, which of course, I've been several times since. The most recent one I did was a guy who wanted to meet this woman in a pub. After some chat and a few drinks, takes her back home only to discover, when he put his hand up her skirt, that she was actually a he. Then, I had to say "I'll shove your head up my skirt and make you suck my big hard cock!" Of course he's moaning and groaning like a good 'un. Tossing himself off for all he's worth. Then he tells me he's going to throw me over the arm of the settee and give me a right good seeing to right up my arse. 'Come on, then you dirty bastard. Give it to me good and 'ard!' That's it, that's him done, it'd had the desired effect and he's gone off satisfied!

Sometimes, as with this one, he knew I was a woman, pretending to be a man being a woman. Grief! Doesn't it get confusing? I felt like poor old Julie Andrews when she played Victor/Victoria.

Being a she-male, however, needed a bit more thought. The tits part was easy to imagine, I'd imagine that from day one, big tits. But tits with cock, now that needed to be well thought out.

When callers come through to book a call, I always say give me five to ten minutes to put your details through, then I'll get the girl to call you. Sometimes, as with this call, I needed time to think about what I had to be. What I usually found to be true in most cases, if you harped on and on about the attribute which inspired them the most, i.e. big tits, hairy pussy or as in this case my big fat bell-end. Then they'd be so turned on by the words you used, they'd believe anything you tell them. Well, we girls know this is the best time to get to grips with a man in the throes of ecstasy.

So, that's what I decided to do. I went on and on about my big cock, how I love wanking it, slowly stroking it up and down the shaft. I'd tell the caller to get down on his knees and suck on my big fat bell-end. Don't forget, you had to use a man's terminology when describing male attributes. Oh, it's complicated stuff, this. No call is straight forward. I told him I'd force it down his throat, push his head down on to it.

"Go on, you fucker, you dirty little cock sucker!" I encouraged. "Swallow that big purple head."

"Get your tits out for me!" he gasps down the phone, wanking himself off furiously.

When you think about it though, a she-male is perfect for a guy, tits and cock! So, this is me as Simone, the she-male.

Now, when it comes to being a transsexual, that's a different kettle of fish altogether. I have to imagine what it would be like to have been a man struggling with the inner turmoil of wanting to be a woman then actually being brave enough to have 'the operation.' For the main part all he wanted to know was what it felt like to have nothing between my legs. No cock or balls hanging down. That for him was the fascination. To pull on my panties or jeans without a bulge trapped inside the item of clothing. So, that's mainly what we talked about. Then one time he came on and wanted to know where I had had the operation done. He was obviously thinking of doing the same thing. Either that, or was he beginning to suss me out, and it was a testing question. Quick as a flash, I said France, just outside Paris. Don't know why, maybe in the recess of my mind I'd heard or read something about cocks being chopped off in France. They used to chop heads off royalty, so why not these sort of heads. Then he asked if I remembered the surgeon's name. Now, he really seemed to be questioning me.

"Ooh, God!" I sweated. "I can't remember. My French isn't very good." That saved me. Now he seemed he was convinced of my gender reversal.

Must have, I still get him coming through for calls, to this day.

Anyway, after the call, I ran down the stairs, I always do my calls in the spare bedroom. I said to Tom, you'll never guess what; I'm a transsexual, now. I told him the tale of the call. He looked at me and said; "Well, you do look as though you could do with a shave!" We had a good chuckle, as always. If you could see what a hairy bitch I am. You'd probably see the funny side, too. And, as it turned out there is a transgender hospital just outside Paris in France. However, I'd hate to think I had a hand in making his decision to go ahead with the 'chop.' But I guess if he felt that's what he wanted to be, then nothing I might say could influence him either way. I don't honestly think anything I'd said could do that, for the most part it's just a fantasy, as with all the other calls.

Curiosity, that's another reason for many of my calls. I really believe that's what it is for this particular caller.

Nobody really wants to do what they talk about as I've said all long. And, of course, it's the same curiosity people have about my line of work that make them want to know more. They love to listen to me being the naughty girl I am who just loves to tell tales.

Finally, this last caller I want to tell you about in my chapter on the things I've been, has got to be one of the more bizarre ones I've ever had to be on a regular basis. He's a one off, like a few of my specialist callers are. But at least it's not too perverted. He's a caller who comes through from one of my Men's Magazines adverts. He's Irish and very well spoken. He wants a mistress to put his wife through obedience class. In other words he wants me to be her dog handler!

Seemingly, she's quite hairy. All over body hair, armpits, fanny, arse and legs the lot!

"She's a dirty dog, Mistress," he would say. "She needs punishing. Why don't you shave her, Mistress? She's a dirty hairy dog. She's a fat lazy bitch. Why don't you call her, Mistress? Her name's Lucy."

Well for some reason, I haven't got a clue why, except for the fact he kept calling her a dog and a bitch, I started to whistle and call, "Here Lucy, come on good girl, come to your Mistress." I'd follow this up with whistling, again several times. "Come on you dirty hairy dog, come when your Mistress whistles." Well, this drove him into an absolute frenzy. I had him cuming all over the place. He loved it!

After that he'd come through quite regularly. I got to know his particular fantasy quite well, as I always do with my 'regs'.

It would always start the same. First, I'd tell him what I looked like, tall, slim, beautiful, big breasts and completely hairless. He was very particular about this last part. Then he'd describe his wife in all her fat, hairy glory. He'd parade my body in front of his wife who he told often to admire my beauty. Yet he was never allowed to touch my beautiful soft smooth skin. He wasn't good enough for that, I had to tease and taunt him with my slender body, all the while stroking myself right in front of him. He'd be saying, "Look at the Mistress, Lucy see how lovely she is."

The best of it was, I was actually closer to his wife's description; fat, hairy, lazy bitch than his imagined Mistress!

Of course, this knowledge was highly amusing to Tom and me.

"If only the poor bastard knew!"

"Well, I'm not telling him, are you?"

I can honestly say whoever I am, I wouldn't want to be anything else other than a sex chat girl. It's the most fun I get, bringing guys off for a living. It certainly gives Tom and me hours of entertainment!

My favourite statement is: "You'll never guess what..."

To which my man always replies. "Here we go, we're off again. What's it to be this time!"

Now, since I started writing six months ago, I always follow up with, "Here's another one for the book..."

Chapter Five

The Lengths I Go To

I must admit, I do pride myself on giving guys a good convincing call. Even Tom can't believe the lengths I go to and he's even seen me do most of them.

I have this one caller who comes through regularly, always has an hour's call at a time, at the cost of fifty pounds a call. And, once or twice, I've had him two or three times in the course of one evening. Again, with him, as with some of the others, I am many girls from Amber and Sophie aged sixteen to Debbie, aged twenty two. It's been really difficult with him because he's always wanted the same sort of soft spoken voice. So, I tell him, like I've had to tell a few others before. We're from the same area. Well, all Liverpudlians sound similar as do Yorkshire lasses and Geordies and so on and so on. In some cases it's very true. Some areas, around the country, people do sound very similar. Give them a good, reasonable sounding excuse and they will swallow it whole. Bless them.

Anyway, the preference with this caller is sound and foot fetish. So, walking around bare foot was the order of the day. There I'd be, wandering around the house and garden, phone close to my feet. Good job he can't smell them, I always think.

He wanted to hear my feet slapping on the laminate flooring and when I told him we had a stone patio, he all but flipped! What you have to remember with this caller is, he's a paraplegic and with him having a foot fetish any sounds made by bare feet used to get him off. He has no feeling from the waist down, which meant he couldn't get an erection but he had tingling feelings up and down his spine, instead of his cock standing up, the hairs on the back of his head stood on end.

He loved telling the girl what to do, like using a make up brush on her toes and feet. Working my way down from my breasts and nipples down to my pussy lips where I was told eventually, to insert the brush handle inside my pussy hole. He always wanted me to go slowly, each toe backwards and forwards endlessly. I would moan and groan faking my pleasure and delight. I had to say in full detail what it all felt like. Sometimes, to vary it a bit, I would tell him what I'd be doing to myself, in slow torturous monotone. Boring myself senseless! He was completely unaware that I could so easily nod off. If I couldn't be bothered to walk around or we had visitors, I used to slap the soles of my feet so that it sounded like my feet slapping on laminate flooring. Well, it must have sounded convincing because he thoroughly enjoyed the call.

Of course, as with long running calls like this it wasn't just about the sounds or the feet. We also used to chat a bit; I got to know about him and his home life. So, in return I had to tell him something about mine. Because I'm just sixteen, I'm not living alone. This is where Tom also changes his persona, he becomes my father! So, I'm now living with my father. Everything has to be well thought out to make the fantasy a bit more realistic.

I remember one time he came through, wanted his hour call as always. Unfortunately, Tom and I intended going out for a meal this particular evening. Up until now, the day had been fairly quiet. A night out was planned and looked forward to, besides there was nothing else to eat in the house. Anyway, I was still to get ready when he came through at seven thirty. His hour call would've taken us to eight thirty, and me still not ready. So, not wanting to let the guy down or turn down the chance of some money. I booked the call with Amy for him. Bear in mind, it's not as though I can offer him another girl, should he request one. There's only me!

This happens many times over with all my regulars. Even on other call backs I've worked on. The owner would give me out as lots of different girls, which unfortunately meant for me, if I wasn't available as Sharon, how could I be available as Irene? So, it was very hard for me to have any time off. This was true of all the guys who had me as different girls. As I've said before, this is the only down side to the job, and it's even worse now, as I'm the only one at all. I have to be available 24/7. I'd have an hour off in the morning to go shopping, most of which now, I do over the internet. The only other time was when we fancied a night out, which was sometimes once every other month. The job pays good money, what can I do now that I'm working for myself? I earn between a hundred and five hundred pounds a day. Yes, a day! So, when we go out it could in fact mean I'd be losing three hundred pounds for that day. Considering I used to get seventy-eight pounds a week as a carer for my mother four years ago. That sort of money becomes too hard to turn down.

Anyway, back to the caller I've got to fob off. Well, it was simple, really. I just told him my aunt had come to visit and we were all going out for a meal. So, I could only chat for half an hour, he'd already paid for his usual hour. And, if he didn't mind, we could have the rest of the chat the next day, when I could tell him all about it. Of course, he was totally blown away by this. He thought it was an excellent idea, meant he could find out more about the real me (yeah, right!). He could have a better rapport with the girl he chats with. Bear in mind he's a fifty year old paraplegic who actually believes that one day he'll come across a teenager who'd be interested enough to want to meet him and after all, I suppose to him knowledge was power. The more he knew about me and all that. So, with that, me and Tom had a good night out and I left him ringing the office in the hope of chatting to one of my other girls only to hear over and over again; "Sorry, all our girls are busy at present, please try later." Thank God for answering machines!

One of my favourite callers is a guy who comes on and pays me twenty five pounds for a thirty minute call and all he does is use the time to get me to check out porno websites for him. He's also one of the callers who used to have several of my other ladies, then decided to give me, as Dee, a go and he's stayed with Dee, ever since.

Sometimes, he wants to do a call while I'm looking at the websites. I tell him what I find and say what they are doing; he gets off on this big time. Other times I can't be bothered or it's too perverse even for me to look at so I make it up. Sometimes, my internet dial up is acting up and I have to invent the websites, anyway. I tell you, imagination is a fantastic thing and it's a good job I'm full of it!

He's another caller who loves disgusting sex chat. Sweaty hairy, pissy fanny lips. He enjoys talking about shagging dirty old grannies dressed in stockings and suspenders, skimpy sexy underwear. He's another one into anal. Tell you what; it's surprising how many guys love talking about it. The websites he likes looking at are grannies with young boys. Come shots, hairy pussies and old dicks with young chicks and, on occasion, girls with dogs and horses. Some, I've even ordered for him. One of the reasons I only pretend to search the internet for adult websites is because I can't bear to look at them! But, on the whole, I still give him a good time with or without the websites. I remember this one time I ordered some DVDs for him and he couldn't wait for me to send them on to him, they'd been a long time coming as I'd forgotten to order them, as usual. Anyway he got me to play one on my DVD player. It was entitled 'Old Lady Dog Lover'. Anyhow, I played it for him. This hideous looking old dear came on the screen in stockings and suspenders and some sort of corset. She started rubbing herself with a vibrator and going (swear to God!) "Heehaw, heehaw, heehaw." And to cap it all I had to describe what she was doing. Then they brought on the fucking dog, panting and grinning, slavering all over the place. Oh, my God! I couldn't believe my eyes. At least the dog looked as though it was enjoying it. Mind you, dogs are dogs, they'd shag owt! I firmly believe, but so would half the blokes in this country!

Well, I was choking back the laughter which stuck in my throat. I thought 'I've got to show Tom!' A short while later he returned from work. I told him about the animal DVDs this caller has ordered. It's not the first time I've ordered them for him. But it's the first time I've had to play them over the phone. We were sitting comfortably, then the DVD starts up. In she comes, the old dear. We've looked at each other, I'm grinning like a Cheshire cat. Tears are welling up in my eyes. Poor Tom has a puzzled expression etched across his face. He can't understand why it looks as though I'm crying, or why this old dear of about sixty-eight has walked onto the TV Screen. His idea of a porn movie is of young nubile blondes prancing across the screen with big tits hitting everyone in the eye. Finally, he asks.

"Is this what this guy's ordered?" I can't speak; I've got my tee-shirt crammed into my mouth. He turns back to the screen as this sound emanates from the direction of the TV. I watch as his eyes widen. She's rolling around on a settee, sucking and licking her vibrator before she rubs it suggestively up and down her crotch. The camera cuts to a close up of her face. Every wrinkle shown in all its glory, the red gash of her mouth splits into a grimace, grin, or whatever it is that's distorting her painted lips. "Aaah," she sighs. "Hee Aaah. Hee haw. Hee haw." She's off again and so am I. I'm writhing about on the sofa in fits of laughter. Talk about who's let the dogs out, it's more like bring on the donkeys!

Tom is still sitting there, mouth agape. Finally, he breaks his silence. "Does he know what he's ordered?" I'm splayed out over our sofa, nodding, shaking more like. I still can't do any more. "Well," he continues, the look of horror gradually diminishing. "I hope he doesn't want his money back."

"Nor do I," I tell him. "I'm the silly bitch who's paid for it!" Anyway he didn't ask for his money back and he still orders his DVDs through me. And you'll be pleased to hear Tom is no longer traumatised from having to watch his old 'granny' pleasuring herself with a vibrator.

As it happens, I had another guy wanting to talk about animal sex. Did I know where I could get some DVDs from? They think we're as perverted as them! But as it happens I did and could.

He'd been going on and on about these bloody animal DVDs for weeks. Wondering how good they were, how explicit. They came from Germany so he wouldn't have to worry about a good script! Anyway, finally, they arrive and I text him at his request. Ooh, the little eager beaver couldn't wait. He was thrilled beyond belief. I thought to myself, no doubt I'll get all the graphic details and he'll go on and on about the bloody things. Anyway, two weeks passed, then three. I guessed he must be glued to the screen. Finally, he rang and yet never said a word about the DVDs. Not even whether or not he'd received them. So, I had to ask. I quote his reply as accuarely as I can recall it;

"The fucking dirty bastards. How could they do that with those dogs, they were licking and sucking and shagging them. Oh," he said. "I was nearly sick; I had to switch it off. I watched about fifteen minutes. Best of it was," he continued. "Every time I saw a woman out with her dog after that. I kept thinking she's not doing it, is she?"

Well, I consoled, grinning from ear to ear. "Obviously some things are best left to the imagination." He never talked about animal sex ever again.

Another extremity comes to mind. He was a first time caller, just recently as it happens. Must have loads of money, he booked call after call. Three hours in all. He wanted a filthy mouthed bitch with an unbelievably dirty mind, and boy did he get one! So, we were well into the chat. He wanted every perversion possible. Seemingly, he loved seeing his wife being shagged by other guys and as it turned out she certainly fucked a few on his behalf. Apparently, his favourite thing was licking another man's spunk out of his wife's pussy. Oh, yes. There are lots of them about. Anyway, it's a Sunday afternoon, the sun was baking, and I've got to water my partner's seed house. He grows plants and sells them for a living. When it's baking hot and he's on a boot or at the market, I water the plants for him. Well, for the most part this is fairly easy. He's got spray lines set up for me to switch on and off after a certain time. The seed house, however, must be watered by hand. I have to say by this time I'm getting concerned, now. He's been on the phone up to now, for two hours and he's booked another hour call. Fifty quid a call, as I've said before, is a hell of a lot of money to turn down.

Anyhow, ten minutes into his third hour the caller decides he wants me to dress just in stockings and suspenders and wander about my garden in the hope of one of my neighbours spotting me. Oh, you get this all the time. A caller will tell you to stand in front of your window and ask if you can see anybody. They want someone to see me. Naturally, I'm making it all up as I go along. Considering we live on two acres of land it's not very likely. Plus, there's a nursery next door, so no one is ever there besides if there was we couldn't be seen. We've got huge trees surrounding the property. We've often gone about the house and grounds with no clothes on.

So, as I said, I'm beginning to panic until I hear him mention the fact he wants me to go on a walk about. All of a sudden my mind goes into overdrive; the seed house, I can get to the seed house. Of course, I'm off and running now. I give him the full treatment. Don't need to pretend any more, can and want desperately to do it! So, there I am, phone in hand walking around for the guy on the other end of the phone. He's asking if anyone can see me. I'm saying no it's a bit quiet at the moment. Then, hit by sudden inspiration, I say to him; "Wait a minute, there's a bit of an industrial estate down at the very bottom of the garden. There's some sort of a garage and mechanics." The beauty of it is there really is a type of industrial estate at the back of our garden. It consists of Aqua Tropics, Some sort of beauty salon and a vehicle repair place. Anyway, I get down there knowing full well it'll be closed. All the time I'm talking to him I'm preparing to water the bloody seed house by changing over the hosepipes.

"Can you see anybody?" He's asking.

"No, no one, yet. Hang on, I'm nearly there." I'm telling him.

Yep, I'm nearly at the seed house. So, there I am almost in position and about to start watering. I think, shit he's going to hear the water. It comes out the spray head in a loud whoosh. Anyway, first off, I've got to tell him there's no one there, because there isn't.

"Aaah," I sigh down the phone trying to sounding disappointed. "I've just remembered!" I tell him. "I bet they've been given the afternoon off because England's playing. I'm sure it was the semi final." He didn't care; he'd got his cock in his hand and was from Canada. "Wait a minute; I call out in glee, can you hear that water? I think the lads are watering in the nursery, next door." Of course, he must have heard it, it was drowning him out! I say into the mouth-piece, "Hang on, they're really close. Yoohoo, yoohoo!" I'm calling out at the top of my voice to be heard over the water gushing against the glass of the seed house. On I go... "Yoohoo yoohoo!" I keep on calling out. Thank god, no one's in next door they'd think I was raving! At last, the watering was coming to an end, so I said. "Ahh, I think they are moving away, they can't hear me over the water."

God! I'd be surprised if anyone could. Finally, the watering had been done and I wandered back to the house and now he wants to listen to dirty movies over the phone....

Thank fuck for that, I'm at least back in the house. Now, I have to fart about looking for pissing dirty DVDs. Anyway, it kept him busy for the rest of the call. And, most importantly the bloody seed house had been watered.

So, thankfully that caller out the way I put the phone on answer and I flopped out on the bed for half an hour. When Tom returned home I told him some guy actually paid me one hundred and fifty pounds to water the seed house. Naturally, as usual, I told him the events of the afternoon call.

"My God," he said in disbelief, "and I have to grow plants all year, load up the van and try to sell the gear for three or four hundred quid, if I'm lucky. All you have to do is potter around the garden."

"Be fair, babe." I teased, "I have to lazy about the house, too." And, of course, lazing about on the bed is where I have to do this next guy I want to tell you about. Good job I've got this fantastically sexy bed to do my calls on, my super king size bed, all the way from America. Plenty of room to roll about on, and believe me for some callers I have to do a lot of rolling around as with this next caller.

He rang through this particular evening, asked who I had available. I gave him a list of names in the age group he was after. This is what I always do with callers who ask what girls are working. I give him one of my friends' names Marie, thirty-two. Along with her description, short, slim, big boobs, with light brown hair and brown eyes.

I put his card details through, successfully, a thirty minute landline at the cost of twenty-seven quid. Give it another five minutes then 'Marie' calls him back. The first thing he asks is what toys have I got. I tell him, a clit stimulator, Chinese balls and a vibrator. When in fact all I've got is a vibrator.

Oh, this is nothing; one caller wanted me to have a clitty bell. What the fuck? I thought. I quickly checked my drawers and came across a light bulb and a jingly sort of bracelet. God knows, don't ask. I have to make it up as I go along. Anyway when I draped the bracelet around the metal part of the bulb it had the desired effect. Naturally, when I 'came' I jingled the bracelet very quickly. "Oh my god darling, you certainly enjoyed that, didn't you, darling!" You can read about this caller in chapter eleven. Believe me; he needs a chapter all to himself!

I digress, back to the caller I was telling you about. The balls didn't make a noise, so that was okay. My clit stimulator, which in fact I did have came in two speeds, fast and pulsate. The normal buzzing sound I said was the vibrator and the pulsating sound I told him was the clit stimulator. To make it sound as though it's going in and out I just roll on and off it. Sound fades, comes back loud. It has the desired effect. Anyway, he's telling me what to do and I simulate doing it moaning and groaning for realism. Then, I can hear what I assume to be a woman I think, moaning somewhere in the background, not very distinctive, but definitely some sort of rhythmic sound. I put it down to a dirty movie he could be playing, most of them do. Even have dirty magazines, so they tell me. Anyway, the sound was like a constant drone; it didn't change pitch or fade. Then I noticed I couldn't hear anything every time he spoke. The sound disappeared altogether. Now, I was really intrigued. There I was rolling around all over the bed, doing all he asked. And all I can do is try to make out if there's someone with him or not. It's not until we were twenty minutes into the call did it suddenly dawn on me, it was him making the noise. He was asthmatic. It was actually him wheezing down the mouth piece. Then, all of a sudden my mobile phone, which is laid on the bed, starts buzzing and beeping, I've got it on silent, you see. I divert my incoming calls to it while I'm taking the call. I had to keep moaning louder and louder every time it went off!

"You're enjoying this," he chimes in.

Yeah, not half. I've got him wheezing in my ear, my stimulator whirring between my legs, squeezing it pretending it's going in and out then the damn mobile phone bleeping and buzzing because some twat is trying to book a call! Oh yes, I really was having the wildest time!

About seven calls I missed in all. That's what happens when you're flying solo. Anyhow, he must have had a great time; he was back the next week to book another hour's call again with the lovely, Marie. We had the whole works, again. The positions he had me in! I was supposed to stand naked, bending over. The balls in my pussy, vibrator up my bum, stimulator trapped in my lips. "Wish I was a peeping Tom," he said.

"How about a window cleaner?" I suggested trying to keep my balance.

"I'll bet he doesn't see this every day!"

We laughed.

By the time we finished the call and I had cum several times. I said to him.

"That's it, me clit's dead and I'm knackered. Ooh, it was good, though. Just a pity I'll be too knackered for my next caller. Me pussy needs the kiss of life. I shall have to make it up."

"Wish I was there to kiss it for you!" He chuckled, we both giggled out of control. Then he said, "That's all right, I'll give you a week or two to recover." And he did, he was back the following week and quite a few weeks thereafter.

The lengths and pretences I go to are nobody's business. Whatever the length that's required of me, I do it. For the most part these calls are great fun. They give me and Tom hours of entertainment long after they've gone. The imagination is a wonderful thing. Just as well I've got the wildest one on line.

I remember when Tom first called me on the PRLs he actually thought I was reading from a script. When I told him that I wrote as a hobby and had in fact written several short stories and a couple of novels. He said, "No wonder you're very descriptive over the phone. You talk as though you are reading."

I guess that when I do the chat, as I call it, more often than not, I know what I'm going to talk about as soon as they mention their particular fantasy. So, in fact I'm writing the story in my mind as I'm telling it. Maybe this was why it always came over as reading a script. But believe me folks, it is all made up.

Chapter Six

Sometimes They Go On for Hours

It is amazing, you know. Some guys do calls for hours at a time. Considering they're charged around fifty quid a time it makes for an expensive night in. I invariably get this one guy who comes through about once or twice a month, booking several hours worth of calls at a time. One night he had four hours' worth of calls some lasting an hour, or maybe half an hour a couple of times, or two hours straight off. I later learned he always did charley while chatting and occasionally, he'd have an escort or two with him. Once or twice I got to speak to one of the so called escorts. (Lucky Me!) The first time, I reckoned it must have really been his wife, doing a bit of role play with him, and why not? It is meant to be fun, after all. But the second time I'm sure it wasn't, the two women sounded completely different. I should know, it's me that's spoken to all of them.

There was something the first girl said which gave it away, she spoke about her Stephen, only a wife would say that. She was pretending to be his fifteen year old niece. Also, it was the way she spoke to him, and when he asked where something was she knew where he'd find it. Now, that was a dead give away, that's definitely the role of the wife. She was supposed to be his fifteen year old niece but she did a worse job of sounding like a teenager than me.

What sort of bloke needed a chat girl on his phone, while watching dirty movies, pretending it was his wife being fucked by her brother and cousin? Oh yes, he was obsessed with that, even though his wife was thirty-two years old. Sometimes, in the make believe video, it's his best mates fucking her. More often than not it was her brother. Occasionally, it's her father while he's shagging his wife's mother. Oh, it's all go in his head! Apparently, she wouldn't let him have anal sex, yet she lets everyone else shag her up the arse. This is another thing he goes on about constantly. So, to re-cap; he has an escort in, watches porn movies and snorts drugs to get himself off! His sexual appetite must have cost him a small fortune. I know it cost him his wife and kids; he told me this the last time he came through. The best of it was, it wasn't enough just to talk about his wife being shagged by all and sundry, he used to dress in her clothes and insert objects up his backside to simulate his wife being shagged up the arse at the same time! I'm sorry but if I had to do this to get myself off, I'd give up on sex. Over the months the talk got more and more bizarre. We touched on every subject imaginable, sometimes with me as Dee but more often than not with me pretending to be a sixteen year old. Seems to me, guys and gals, his whole life was one big pretence!

I know long lengthy calls mean plenty of money, but when you've had the same guy time and time again you become complacent. The fantasy is nearly always the same and because he thinks you're a different girl you have to listen to the same sodding story over and over, again! It all becomes mind numbingly boring. Also, as with all calls longer than twenty minutes, I always did it laid down on the bed. This, coupled with the fact that I've been up most of the previous night taking calls, I'm pretty much shagged out. So, unfortunately, I tend to nod off. The first I know of it is someone somewhere in the distant recess of my sleepy mind, shouting,

"Hello. Hello, anyone there? Can you hear me?" To which I sometimes reply, "Oh, sorry. I was listening to what you were saying." Or, I might say, "God! This bloody phone! Yes, I can hear you now." Whatever it takes to convince them I'm awake. Well, why not, I can convince them of everything else.

When I did the Premium Rate Lines, the calls came through quick and fast. Sometimes I'd do them while laid next to my partner, Tom. I could only do this of course, out of his selling season, he's a market trader, in which case it didn't matter if I disturbed him or not, he was unconscious! If he was snoring, however, I'd have to go in to the other bedroom. Mind you, it was lucky for me he was beside me sometimes, especially if I received a call in the middle of the night. The giveaway for him he says is when he hears me mention food. Seemingly, when I'm drifting off, I'd start talking about food. When he heard the word chocolate, this one night, he knew the caller was in trouble and he'd nudge me awake. We'd often laugh, wondering what the poor caller on the other end of the line made of my mad midnight ramblings.

I had a new guy come through a couple of weeks ago, an hour call. Unfortunately, it was really hot this particular day and I was finding it very hard to stay awake. Yet again, a victim of late night wankers! He had a low, mellow voice which had me drifting off in next to no time. Yes, I know what you're thinking; it's amazing how I get guys coming back, at all. Guess what, readers? So am I! Anyway, I check the time on the phone, seventeen minutes into the call. On he goes, and I lie there listening. I'm obviously moaning and groaning in the right places. I look at the phone, again. All of a sudden we're forty four minutes into the hour call. I'm trying to clear my mind and I can hear him saying, "You sounded like you had a good time." I'm laid there trying to work out where the time's gone. I could have sworn blind that only a couple of minutes have passed. Now, I'm trying to remember what I've said. Fuck knows what he's been talking about, because I don't! Anyway, I bring myself back to the call and finish him off.

"You really enjoyed that, didn't you?" he said.

Stifling a yawn and stretching I tell him, "It was the best call I've had in a while."

"I love pleasing women," he said, happy in the knowledge he's satisfied the girl on the other end of the line. 'Well, babe,' I thought, 'you certainly pleased me, all right. I had a lovely kip.'

It's wrong, I know, but what else is a girl to do. Another regular who comes through has the same effect on me. I think it's because they do all the chat, I just have to lie and listen. I'm not using my brain so I just switch off.

Some poor bloke might come through in the middle of the night to book a call. Even as I take the details, I'm nodding off. I could just imagine the next day. The poor bastard must've been sat there with his cock in his hand waiting for some dirty bitch to help him relieve himself. Unfortunately, what often happens, silly old me would fall asleep leaving the phone off the hook. Then I bet the poor caller would be trying to get through to find out where his call was, gradually losing the strength in his knob. I often wondered if he lost the will to go on at all worrying about whether or not I'd taken money off his card and then not given him his call. Am I wicked? You betcha!

Don't get me wrong not all calls are tedious; sometimes we have a bit of a chat. Tell each other jokes. One day this regular came on and we chatted about my cats and dog. I don't know how we got onto the subject. I must have spent about fifteen minutes of his time telling him all about them. Then spent further twenty minutes trying to talk him into getting a dog. In fact there was only about fifteen minutes of the call left when I realised we hadn't done the sex chat. Come to think of it I don't think we did it at all that time. I guess I must be doing something right, he still comes back. He has me as Val, sixty-three.

Apparently, this guy's partner left him soon after she gave birth to their son. There were no ill feelings, it was just a mistake to stay together. However, she didn't deprive him of his son. In fact when the son grew up he often stayed with his father, who's never married by the way. The chat with him was about his son, and his girlfriend. Although the son and girlfriend have a place together, they often went round his father's house for a shag, and they'd shag for a couple of hours. Of course as you can imagine with him being there at the same time, he could hear them. One time he'd gone to the bog and returned only to find his son being sucked off by his girlfriend. So, as you can guess, it became an obsession with the father, hearing them shagging all the time made him terrifically horny. Sometimes when we did the call, I had to pretend to be the girlfriend and catch the father wanking off. She's just left the bedroom where she'd been fucking his son. Then she'd get fucked by his father. As I said earlier, for the most part of the hour call we'd just have a good chat and a bit of a laugh in between him telling what the son and girlfriend got up to. What I did find a bit odd was, if they had a place of their own, why did they have to go round to his father's house for sex? It might just be me, but I find that a little strange. Still, takes all kinds.

Not all callers go on for hours and hours continually; another type of caller is the one who books ten minutes calls one after another. This particular guy I feel I have to mention, he's actually an old regular of mine, he used my company at the beginning when I first started up. I had him through again, recently, a couple of weeks ago. I guess he must have recovered a lot quicker this time. Well, he was an alcoholic. Every time he fell off the wagon, he called a sex chat line for a mistress to abuse him for being so weak. When he rang me the first time it was because he had fallen off the wagon. He was quite chatty at the beginning, told me all about himself. That he was a nice guy, really, just felt the need to abuse himself, every now and again. For some reason his obsession was his own backside and the backsides of large ladies. So, this was the topic of conversation. Well, that and me being his mistress, which was any girl available for me to do him as a mistress.

Anyway, he had a smelly, pooy bum, his words. He would smell it over the phone while we chatted. I could hear him sniffing his fingers. I'd often tell him to put his finger up it and sniff it to see just how smelly it was. Yes, I know, I can be just as disgusting as the callers. Come on, be honest I'd have to be as perverted as them to do half these calls. Pretend to be, at least. Yes, I must admit I do get a perverse kick out of doing the most disgusting and obscene calls. I like to see how dirty they are prepared to go. I have actually had some men say to me that I'm too dirty for them. There's just no accounting for taste! On the other hand, when I'm being a sweet young teenager, they say I can't talk dirty to you, you sound too nice. However, they inform me, I will have a good toss off later tonight thinking about your sexy voice. I think to myself, get your cock out you pathetic little wanker and toss yourself off! Oh, I'm a dirty filthy bitch.

Anyhow, back to this guy who wants to be abused. Boy, did I abuse him. Poor Tom was horrified at what I made him do. Made him think twice about the girl he was shacked up with. Well, if they want to be dirty disgusting pigs, let's have a little fun with it, that's what I say. I have to admit, even I shock myself. The worst thing I made him do was, pick his nose and stick the boogies up his arse. I'm sorry to say I absolutely howled at this. I literally peed myself. The dirty fucker actually did it! Tom was completely gob smacked at this. I'd sunk to the lowest of the low and thanks to me so did the caller. It became an obsession, shoving things up his arse. The odd thing was, he only ever booked a ten minute call, but he would do this between ten and twenty times a day. It must have cost him a small fortune. He went through credit cards like no body's business. I'm ashamed to say, I even got him to the stage of him showing off his backside in public. The local corner shop was his favourite exposure place, that and his back garden. I used to make him go out there with the pretence of him doing some weeding, say a very nice, "Good afternoon," to his neighbours, then told him to pull down his shorts as he was bending over to do the weeding. I'm sorry, but I thought it was absolutely fucking hilarious. I still have a good chuckle to myself to this day. Well, serves the arsehole right! He shouldn't have been so weak in the first place. I just had a little fun, is all. This went on for a couple of months, I must admit, even I felt sorry for the guy in the end. Every time he came through, he got worse and worse. Until in the end it was just me doing the calls with him. I'd keep on and on about him seeking help.

Because he did, bless him. He did need help. Yes, I had my money out of him and my entertainment but when I realised how bad he was getting I put a stop to it. When he came through towards the end I just chatted with him. Talked about what was troubling him and yes, I did finally talk him into seeking help. He never came through, again for almost a year. He called me a few times over a couple of weeks, just recently. But I guess it must have been enough to cure him because he never came back again. And, I do really hope for his sake he doesn't because he really was a very nice guy, with not such a nice problem.

Chapter Seven

They Get The Urge In The Oddest Places

You cannot imagine for one minute where some of the guys are when they do a call. I don't believe it half the time myself, but then again, I wouldn't put it past any of the dirty bastards that come through.

Calling from the office. Yes, you're probably thinking, that wouldn't surprise you. But how about him waiting for his boss and a few of his colleagues to join him for a meeting! This one guy came through and actually said he may have to cut short the call because he was expecting his boss and some colleagues coming in to his office at any minute. He even gave me a running commentary of when they were approaching. "I can hear them in the next room, they're all gathering there before they come through. Carry on." he encouraged. I continued with the chat for another couple of minutes. "Wait a minute." I stopped, imagining what must be going on. I knew from what he said that he was actually sat at his desk with his cock in his hand, wanking off. No one could see his cock from the doorway, he told me as much. Obviously it was the thrill of getting caught that turned him on. Then, I heard voices in the distance.

"They're opening the door. I'm just about to come." He told me. I heard a muffled groan, just as the voices sounded a little closer. A slight sigh escaped over the mouth-piece. "I've got to go, now. Thanks, bye."

I reckon he must have been sat there with his cock still out all through the meeting with spunk dripping off the end of his knob. The absolutely dirty bastard! Well, he must have. He certainly didn't have time to put it away. They were in the office, talking as he was saying, "Thanks. Bye!" Unbelievable? They all are.

Sitting in their cars. Yes, this is quite common. They are out on the road feeling horny. His little man is rearing his ugly head in search of some attention. He comes across a lay-by pulls in, rings me to help him have a pull on his knob. This is quite the norm, nothing usual about this.

What about, you've got family round for a weekly visit and you get the horn. What's a guy to do? I know I'll nip out to the car parked in the driveway. Get my knob out make a quick phone call and have a toss. Anyone could come looking for you but what the hell. The wife, the mother-in-law, even your teenage son or daughter. The neighbours, a stranger or absolutely anyone of a thousand people could approach the car. Is it dark? Is it fuck! It's five in the afternoon. I know they get off at the possibility of getting caught. Some of them are just obscene.

Calling from home, sitting downstairs in a comfy armchair. Most do, most call and they're in their sitting room. This is okay; this is normal, nothing risky in that. No? Until you can hear a woman shouting, "Where are you, what you doing?"

"I'll be up in a minute, love! It's alright," he's telling me. "She'll go back to bed in a minute." He shouts out, his mouth away from the phone. "Just getting a drink, love!" So, we continue with the chat. Now, what you must appreciate, I'm more on edge than he obviously is. So, what do we talk about during these nerve racking calls, I haven't got a clue. I can't tell you what we are talking about; I'm not concentrating on the chat. I'm listening out for his wife. So, when I say we continue with the chat it's because I've lost the plot. That's the most detail I can give you.

Next thing, the phone's gone dead. She's obviously in need of a drink herself and is clumping down the stairs. Me, I just lie there smiling to myself, imagining she caught him with his cock out. I sometimes wonder if she's annoyed at finding him like that, having a crafty toss. Or, is she amazed he can still get it hard because she can't remember the last time she's seen it!

You may think that was a close call. There have been quite a few over the years I've been doing the chat lines, I can tell you. However, none as close as this next caller I want to tell you about. It was close alright, closer that you could ever dream possible but close, in a different way.

It's a dead giveaway when they come on the phone, whispering. This one guy was speaking so low, I could hardly hear him. "Can you speak up a bit?" I asked, "I can barely catch a word you are saying."

How do we do these sorts of calls in such low hushed tones you may be wondering, that's easy, we do all the chat. But first, I have to at least find out what he wants to talk about. I swear on my mother's life this was his reply. "I can't speak any louder; I'm laid next to the wife! You talk."

Oh, my God! Do we really sleep that soundly? Good Lord, it's one thing not knowing what they get up to behind our backs. But fuck me, not laid beside us! The audacity of the bastard!

Does this take the biscuit? You'd think so, wouldn't you? But no, there's one more call to really blow our socks off. We're back to the guy, a different guy, calling again in the middle of the night. Once more, we are in the middle of the call and I can hear a woman calling in the distance. Whether or not he's heard her I have no idea. He doesn't acknowledge he's heard her. He's talking to me, still doing the call. I take it he's wanking, he doesn't have to be, but they usually are. Then I heard clearly, a very angry woman call out. "Who you talking to down there?"

He said to me. "Ignore her; she's in a strop, as usual." They'd had words at some point during the night, which was obvious. Maybe he was doing this out of spite. Some do. Next thing, she's screaming at him. "Are you talking to one of them dirty bitches on the phone, again?" A barrage of obscenities floods the air.

Amazingly, the fucker is still talking to me. "Ignore the bitch, she'll have a rant then she'll calm down." All this time he's never said a word to her; he's still talking to me.

Admittedly, that's all we are doing now, is talking. "She'll go back to bed in a minute." Oh, but she doesn't. Next thing, she's obviously come into the room. I can hear her hitting him. She's screaming at him, calling him all the names under the sun. And still he doesn't hang up. Of course, I'm spellbound, compelled to listen to what was happening at the other end of the line. Finally, I break my silence. She's telling him, this is the last straw. She was packing her bags and clearing off, she'd had enough.

"Hadn't you better go after her?"I ask. Can you believe we're still having any sort of a conversation at all! What on earth was he, or me, thinking of? Next I hear, "Where's the car keys?" Here I am telling him she's serious, trying desperately to make him realise she's really fucking off and he's not saying a thing. She's doing her pieces at him and he's obviously still sat there with the phone in his hand. Finally, I hear a door slam, followed by silence.

"She meant it," I told him.

"Nah, she'll be back." Quite calmly, he settles himself back into the chat.

I've often wondered over the weeks, whether or not she came back. I sometimes think he did it on purpose to get rid of her. It obviously wasn't the first time he'd done it. She knew what he was doing.

I know it takes all sorts to make a world and you get most of them come on the phone line. And, I know what I do for a living must shock people most times and I can't imagine for one minute what sort of men use this service from time to time. There are weirdos and there are sickos, they go with the territory, but cruel unfeeling bastards, they just take the piss.

And finally, a close call of a completely different kind. It happens not too often and even though I'm more aware of it than I used to be at the beginning, it still catches me off guard. I go to dial the number, wait patiently for a reply then the wife answers the phone. The first time this happened I was working for another company. I was completely flummoxed; I quickly hung up the phone. We always withhold our number so the caller doesn't get our home phone number. That's a blessing two fold when the missus answers. However, what I do now is, I ask for the girl I'm meant to be. If I'm Sharon I ask for Sharon and so on. And on the very unlucky occasion the woman on the other end of the line says she is she, then I check the phone number with her and as I always have the number in front of me I usually say the last digit incorrectly. After all I'd hate the little wanker to be found out! In actual fact, I'd hate to be the one she finds out from.

In this line of work you have to be ready for every eventuality. I answered my phone the other day and for a change no one spoke. I did as I always do nowadays as I'm an old hand at the silent treatment; I repeated my little rehearsed speech louder and dripping with stupidity ,"Hello, live call back." To which they always hang up. I know I sound like a bitch but it's the only way to treat the time wasters, they are preventing the genuine wankers from getting through.

Anyway the phone rang again, this time a woman's voice came over the line. "Oh, hello I'm just checking out this number, it's appeared quite a few times on our phone bill."

"Did you ring a moment ago? Sorry, I thought it was some idiot on the line. This number appeared on your phone bill?" I paused, wondering how to continue. It was obviously some poor woman whose sad excuse for a husband has been using my company. "It's a residential line," I told her.

"What, like an elderly people's home?"

I chuckled, "No, it's my home number."

"I thought a number starting with 0870 is always a business number."

"Oh, it was a business line?" I queried, sounding a bit dumb. "In that case you've come through on my husband's business line."

"Right, and what business is he in. It could be a business number to do with my husband's work. I did think it could be that."

For once I decided to tell the truth, don't know why, but there you go, I did. "My husband is a plant worker; he grows and sells plants for a living."

"That explains it!" Relief flooded down the phone, from both ends. "It is to do with my husband's business, after all. Thanks for clearing that up for me."

She didn't say exactly what his business was and I didn't care either way. I guess you might say; saved, again!

I couldn't believe my luck! When Tom came in for lunch, I told him all about it. "See," I said, "it pays to tell the truth, sometimes! Not too often, though."

Chapter Eight

Making Their Fantasies A Reality

For the main part that's what it's about. I'm talking about role play. Not just naughty nurses or schoolgirls but actually making them believe what you say is what you do. A lot of guys, although they know it's a fantasy chat line they've come through on, want to believe they are talking to women who have actually experienced what they are talking about. Yeah, right. As if we as perverted as them!

What makes me pee, is when they ask me, "Do you know if they (the company, they've come through on) takes on guys to talk to women? I could do this for a living, talk about dirty sex all day." I chuckle to myself and think. Yeah, that would be right, us paying you to talk about sex. Only blokes are stupid enough to pay women to talk to them about sex. Let's face it; why would we pay to talk to them about sex! They never listen to us when we talk to them about everyday things, anyway, let alone know what turns us on. It's no wonder they come through on these lines. They live in a fantasy world!

I've had this regular through since almost day one of my starting out on my own. His thing is cat fights. As it is, I get quite a few guys wanting cat fights. So, thanks to him I'm quite good at it, now. Some are more violent than others. His chat always starts the same. We are in this hot room, no windows, no furniture, nothing. He's sat on the floor watching me and this other woman getting all worked up for the fight we're about to get into. For him, the thing that does it is the description of me and the other woman. I give him the description of my mate Christine, large voluptuous lady in her late forties. She has long, straight, brown hair, with brown eyes. Large pendulous breasts, round swollen tummy, big fat round arse. By this time, except for the tits, I'm describing myself. He's into really big ladies. Funnily enough, quite a few of my callers are. Then I tell him what she, the other woman, looks like. She's blonde, long wavy hair, brown eyes because she's a dyed blonde. She has to be, because we both have to have big bushy armpits and big fat hairy fannies, the hair must be growing down our inner thighs. Along with the rest of our bodies. All the while I'm telling him this, I can hear him moaning and groaning.

As I say, we are stood facing each other, ready to do battle. We are both completely naked except for our strappy high heel shoes, little ankle bracelets and long dangly earrings. Most of this description is at his request. Our chunky ringed fingers and long red painted talons.

"Your eyes travel up our bodies," I'm saying, low and breathy. "From our taut calf muscles up to our nut crushing thighs. You can see the hair sticking out from between our fat sweaty, hairy pussy lips. You can see and smell our glistening, pissy pubic hair. See how our period blood has collected in our lips and has matted our pussy hair." Of course as soon as I mention the word blood it sends him into a groaning frenzy. I continue by saying, "Your eyes travel up to our large pendulous breasts. Big rubbery nipples standing out, erect. See the light reflecting in our long dangly earrings. You watch mesmerised as the beads of sweat form on our faces and slowly trickle down our bodies. Now we face each other squatting like sumo wrestlers. Slowly, the blood drips from our gaping pussy lips. It starts to drip faster as the sweat running down the cracks of our arses mingling with the piss and blood of our fanny hair."

Then we kick two tons of shit out of each other and he goes off a very happy bunny. Sometimes he likes us to go down on each other in a sixty-nine. Licking all the above mentioned out of each other. The best of it is though, he actually believes I or any woman could be interested in doing this. And he wonders why I don't meet up!

The most amazing thing is we've been doing this same fantasy for eighteen months, now. Two or three times just about every single week, except when he goes away on holiday, for over a year and a half and it is still the exact same fantasy. The age of my opponent might change but the bloody cat fight never does, the emphasis is on the *bloody!*

Another guy's reality/fantasy is me as Pam, selling my body for ciggies and alcohol. I even have to describe my living accommodation as a bedsit with dirty ashtrays and empty vodka bottles lying around. I'm a dirty old whore in my late fifties who is used for sex by all and sundry. Especially, by guys in the ethnic minority who own corner shops. He absolutely loves it when I tell him my pussy is still full from the night before and how I bet he'd love to be inside me with all that juice running out.

Also, I've sent him a pair of my panties, filled with all sorts, thanks to Tom. Well, that's what he asked for and he is paying. Plus, a couple of pictures, I scanned them from an old dirty magazine of Tom's. He was thrilled to bits when he received them.

I light up and puff away furiously on imaginary cigarettes. I even cough and swear I'm going to pack the fucking fags ups. Which I did ten years ago, but you see, it all adds to the authenticity of the call.

Me being their wives is another type of reality/fantasy chat. They tell me what their wife looks like and what they'd be wearing, and then I have to take on that persona along with the wife's name and make the fantasy real. He wants us to be in a hotel. I'm ready before him so I go down to the bar to wait for him. When he joins me, I'm flirting with the barman. After his shift ends, this is always in about ten minutes. He comes up to my room to fuck me; where unbeknown to the barman my husband will be in a discreet corner to watch him fuck the arse off me.

These are all guys who want to see their wives being shagged by other men. Some, even gang banged! It turns them on to see their wives taking big cocks. I always think to myself, tell you what mate, it would turn me on to take big cock, too!

Another regular comes through, usually in the middle of the night, dressed as a little French Maid. He always starts the same, describes what he's wearing. Then tells me he's been a naughty girl, spying on me in the stables with the young groom. Then he wants me to fuck his arse with a strap-on. And all the time I can hear his vibrator buzzing away. Then he says. "Oh, yes, Mistress. It's going in, it's going in. Yeeehhss. Thank you very much, Mistress. Good night." That's him done.

As Tom would say, "Another satisfied customer?" You betcha!

I had this one guy keep ringing the latest advert I placed in the daily newspaper. The ad referred to ladies who had fallen from grace. Amazingly, there are few similar ads in the paper: Angels who speak naughtily and young angels. So why copy? I didn't they did. But that's how it goes. Sometimes though, I copy them. My new company name came about on account of a particular caller who I've dedicated a whole chapter to, Chapter Eleven. I felt the name was appropriate to his calling, a man of the cloth. I wanted to attract him to my company and obviously, it did.

So anyway, this new guy keeps ringing the advert. He'd ask a couple of questions, then off he'd go. I say to Tom, another time waster. We do get quite a lot of them.

I came back from the shop the other day and Tom pounced on me.

"For fuck's sake that pissing phone has been ringing off the hook. If you hadn't have come back next time it rang, I'd have answered it myself and told the arsehole to fuck off!"

I picked it up, checked the missed call list and recognised the number. It was this recent time waster. Of course, when I told Tom he was not a happy bunny, to say the least. He had rung twenty times, one after another. Why they keep ringing and ringing when they've heard a message telling them 'all our girls are busy at the moment' amazes me but they do this regularly. Anyway, I was about to unpack the shopping when the phone went, again.

It was him. "Did you just call me?" he asked.

"No." Why the fuck would I be calling him!? Then he said the oddest thing.

"Oh, I thought you wanted more details." I just glared in astonishment at the phone like it had spoken some sort of gibberish, but that somehow or other I understood it.

"Why would I ring you?"

"Oh, oh. Sorry, my mistake."

Weird fucker! Oh my god! You do get them and how.

That night we had just got into bed and the phone went.

"Hey up," I said to Tom, "It's your mate from this afternoon. The time waster!"

However, this time he asked me a few questions; how much, what time do you close, what age girls. I told him all the answers. He rang off. Not twenty minutes later, he rang and asked again. This happened on and off all the next day.

I said, "Fuck me! If you don't know by now you never will, you arsehole." Don't worry, I'd already hung up. I always comment after some tosser has been through. Gets the frustration off my chest!

That night I had a late call and fell asleep in the bed I bought while working for the PRLs, a beautiful ornate bedstead. I mentioned it earlier. It was one of those old fashioned high ones. The headboard spans a whopping seven foot wide and five foot high. I couldn't get rid of it when I moved in with Tom. I'd only had it four months. So, I made him get rid of his old spare bed, so I could put mine in. Well, it was my office, after all! I'd often do this if it was really late, sleep in my special bed. Anyway, I'd just got back into bed with Tom who was still asleep, when the phone went. Good God Almighty! It's him, again.

Anyway amazingly, this time he actually booked a ten minute call with a sixteen year old. He wanted one who sounded young and innocent. I gave him Sophie.

I don't know why, but certain names make me sound differently on the phone. When I do, for example, Amber, she always comes across as a cheeky little minx. Yet, for guys wanting a young, submissive type I can play this better with Sophie. It's a gentle sounding name, for a gently spoken girl.

I took a while ringing him back - well he had been wasting my time the last three days. Sometimes I do it to make it look as though they really are waiting for the girl to ring and that maybe it's because we're busy. Sometimes, when they ring to see where their call is, I'll say, "God! I'll bet the silly bitch has copied the number down wrong, I'll ring her." Of course, all this comes in handy when the calls are backed up and I've got several guys to ring. But, I did it to him just to be an arsehole back.

Finally, 'Sophie' rings him.

"Is that Sophie?" he asks. "Can we do a role play?" I say, of course, to both.

"Right, you're a waitress in this hotel. You're still at school but you are working to earn money for college. You are totally young and innocent. You are wearing, a black skirt with a white blouse and a little white apron with black tights." He had the broadest cockney accent, real blokey, rough sounding and coarse. 'Cor blimey, Guv,' type. Anyway, seemingly he wanted to ring down for room service late at night, requesting a bottle of champagne and two glasses. He asked me if I knew a woman off the telly called, Carol Smilie. Which, I did. A somewhat odd question, but as usual, you go along with them. That's what we do.

I knocked on the fantasy door, he said to come in. What happened next you will never guess in a million years? Swear on my mother's life everything I tell you, the reader, is true. He was 'Carol Smilie.' I had to pretend as part of the fantasy, that he was Carol Smilie. (Sorry, Carol) Not only that, he wanted to seduce me as Carol Smilie! And, he did. He not only wanted to seduce me as Carol Smilie but he was going to pay me to do it. He ended the call as he rubbed her pussy hard and fast against mine. "Beg me for more!" he grunted down the phone. So I did and he/she gave me more. Finally, Carol came all over phone and she left completely satisfied.

Next morning she was back making the usual enquiries. I shouted out to Tom. "Hey, up. It's Carol Smilie, again. Wants to know the price of a fifteen minute call."

"She had a good time, then?" Tom said, stating the obvious.

I guess he must have had a great time, he's been back as a girl off Blue Peter and a female stripper. The fantasy is pretty much the same he seduces the young girl, him as a woman. The odd thing is though we have to go through the same performance of booking a call. He still makes the same enquiries, asking the same questions days before he actually books a call. It can go on for as long as a couple of weeks before he finally books a call. He's back, now as Carol Smilie. I've got a lot more patience with him, now. He's very polite and I'm very accommodating, then he will eventually book a call and everyone's happy.

Another regular caller who comes through once or twice every six weeks or so, books a call to his hotel room. Yes, there are a few who do this. This is okay, as a rule, provided there is someone on reception to answer the phone. Anyway, this guy wants a dominatrix with a difference; he wants me to be a lesbian Dom. He wants me to seduce a young innocent girl usually, and the girl must be an employee of mine. I'm Debbie, twenty-six and the victim is an eighteen year old office assistant. I have to go on some business meeting away somewhere and insist she accompanies me. Of course it's just an evil ploy to have my wicked way with her. To force her into having oral sex with me and turn her into a slut-loving pussy licker, like myself. To shag her senseless with my big strap-on and make her my sex slave. It's nice to have a normal fantasy, once in a while.

Another regular who comes through two or three times a month, always books a thirty minute call with any girl aged between twenty and thirty. Sometimes he wants to be in control and other times he wants to be controlled. Either way, the fantasies are nearly always the same.

The first time he came through, I gave him Debbie and he told her the fantasy he was after. Apparently, he received an invitation to the opening of a new unisex salon. First haircut free and he'd come to claim his free haircut. I was to show him to the barber's chair and my girls were to secure him into the chair with manacles around his wrists and ankles amidst his protests and him asking why does he need securing in this manner. I have to say it's because we don't want any sudden movements from him and it's to protect my girls from unwelcome groping. It was for his safety as well as theirs. This, of course appeased him.

Then I'd follow this up by cutting off his trousers. Him frantically protesting and screaming at us to stop this nonsense at once. We naturally ignore his pleas and proceed to strip him of his lower garments. Then, much to his horror, we'd start to shave his cock and balls. Slowly, revealing his knob. Of course, all the time he's begging us not to do something, we would go right ahead and do it. All the time I am to tell him I'm filming the exposure of his knob and have a girl take close up pictures of his knob being exposed.

It was his words, because it was his fantasy. His knob being on display and pulling his foreskin right back for the entire world to see!

As I said earlier, sometimes he did the controlling. The fantasy would start with the girl who was doing the call with him answering an advert to do some modelling. Usually, the modelling involved shaving her pussy and exposing her lips and clitty to the world. Again, he would be filming and taking close up pictures of it all taking place. I would have to dress in a very short skirt which was more like a belt, revealing everything and a blouse that allowed my big tits to be on display. I had to climb onto this stool with a huge vibrator attached to it, a mechanical one and he would press the button on the remote control and have me writhing about in a frenzy, clit sticking out like a chapel hat peg. Exposure of certain body parts beyond our control was his thing.

He is a really nice guy to do, well spoken. He's polite and a gentleman. Never swears, just a gentle fantasy with a gentle guy with a specific sexual desire.

It could be argued, I suppose, that we are lying to these poor suckers who come on line expecting God knows what from us. We do do a very good job of convincing them that we are what they want us to be. At the end of the day, if they really want to believe what we say is true, that's up to them. We are and always will be a fantasy line and that's what we advertise ourselves as. At the same time, they make my life a whole lot more interesting and I hope I do the same for them.

Chapter Nine

Dressing for the Occasion

Although we're usually asked what we are wearing, sometimes the caller will ask when he books the call, "Can she be wearing...?" That's not really what this chapter is about. It's about guys who dress up when they do the call with us. I get this one caller who come through and he will change his clothes two or three times a night. He will chat with the lovely eighteen year old Debbie for ten minutes, he'll tell her what he's wearing in great detail, he'll do the call with her, and then he'll say, "I'll call you back as soon as I've changed." He never comes until the third or fourth call, he likes to build it up and build it up. It turns out he actually used to be a boxer. He must have a good body on him, though, because he goes to the gym six times a week and now does kick-boxing.

He's a lovely bloke to talk to, he just loves dressing up in women's clothes, and especially telling you what he's wearing down to the last detail. Sometimes he's a naughty schoolgirl complete with a blonde plaited wig and satchel. Naturally, when he's a schoolgirl he likes me to be one. I always start the chat by asking him what he's wearing instead of the other way round. He'll start by telling me he's got red lacy topped stockings, red suspender belt, red lacy bra with chicken fillets stuffed inside. A blonde girly wig, red lipstick and six inch black stilettos and that he's feeling very sexy, tonight.

To which I always reply in my sexy sounding eighteen year old voice. "Mmmm, you sound really sexy, baby." And I truly think he does. He's got a very sexy soft spoken voice with a bit of a Geordie accent, which is my favourite accent. Then, I proceed to tell him what I'm wearing. If he's in red, I'm in black. If he's in white, I'm in red. And, if he's in black, I'm in white. I usually make sure I'm wearing something nice and sexy for him. Well, I can tell him whatever I like; I could be naked for all he knows. Which I'm sure he wouldn't mind.

He used to do the chat with most of my younger girls. Now, he's settled on Debbie and now she's the only person he'll ask for.

When we are being schoolgirls, he likes to think of the two of us seducing a teacher. We're two very naughty girls turning the teacher on, making his big cock hard. He himself has what he calls a girly cock; he keeps it tucked inside his panties. Though, God know why he calls it a girly cock, he informed me long ago that's he's got a nine inch cock! Don't misunderstand me, he's not gay, he's bi. He just loves sucking cock. And, who can blame him! However, he likes a girl with him to share the cock. He wouldn't dream of going with a man unless there's a girl with them.

What never fails to amaze me is how they seem to settle on one girl. Considering it's always me. Is it the voice, the description, age? What? I'm completely mystified. Don't get me wrong there are always the floaters; guys who never settle with one girl, or company, for that matter. I've done the same guys through my company that I've done on all the different companies I've worked for. So they should, they should try a few out. But what makes one guy stick to a certain girl? I've had guys who have had me as one sixteen year old for quite a while. They'll come through ask for another, and then they say the second girl was the best they've ever had.

I'm always amazed when they stick with me at all. Like Tom says, some guys like to stick with what they know. Maybe that's how he's come to be stuck with me. Better the devil you know! He's only ever done one chat line, and poor bastard found me. He says I've cured him. Never, ever again will he phone another chat line. Yeah, I always remind him, look what happened the first time. This is what you get for meeting up with someone you don't know, you can't get rid of them!

Anyhow, I digress. Dressing for the occasion, can bring out some weird and wonderful people on these phone lines. Another guy I've had many times, always as a different girl, he comes through for the same fantasy every time. He's into rubber raincoats. The fantasy starts with him knocking on my door, wearing his mackintosh. He's come for a night of lust.

"What are you wearing under your rubber rain coat?" He breathes heavily with anticipation down the phone. "I'm wearing black sheer stockings on my long slender legs." My husky voice informs him. "A black lacy sexy suspender belt and a black skimpy thong which cuts right into my silken hairy pussy lips."

"Does it go right up the crack of your arse?" his gruff sounding voice with a tinge of Welsh enquires.

"Oh, yes, babe. It's rubbing right against it. My pussy lips are dripping."

"Have you got a peephole bra on?"

"Yes," I sigh, lustfully. "A black lacy one and my big rubbery nipples are poking out. I'm rubbing them as we speak."

Notice we use the word 'rubber' a fair bit. That's what does it for him. Rubbery and rubbing. It heightens the sexual tension. He then goes on to tell me that he wants to fuck me in my rubber raincoat, but first he wants to rub the end of his cock against my raincoat. He wants to feel the coolness of the rubber pressing against his hard helmet while his fingers delve into the heat of my wet pussy.

Although he's booked a fifteen minute call all this talk of rubber gets him off in less than ten minutes! Frees me for my next call. Forward thinking, I believe it's called.

Some guys actually come on line wearing their wives' clothes. Not just the bra, panties, stockings and suspenders. They are also wearing her mini skirt and top. This one particular guy comes through dressed like this, not only does he want to dress like her he wants to fuck himself like his wife gets fucked. Not just with a dildo, but with a carrot or cucumber. Sometimes even a wine bottle. If you ask me you need a lot of bottle to fuck yourself with one of them!

One particular caller not only dresses like a little girl, he likes to be called Susan. I was mummy Elaine. I used to do him for another company. He would ask when I called him, "Is it time for bed, mummy?" Or, "Is it time to get ready for school, mummy?" Sometimes he likes me to take the imitative. I'd be collecting him from school. Maybe we'd be going shopping for new white panties. Occasionally, we'd take a trip to the park where all the men would be looking at him/her. And I had to make a point of saying this. If he was on the swing, some man would be trying to look up her skirt.

When we're getting ready for bed, I have to say I was washing her between her legs. "Is that nice, mummy's little darling?"

"Oh yes, mummy, rub a bit faster."

'Susan' always likes to be towelled dry with a big fluffy white towel, creamed, then powdered before putting her nappy on. What twelve year old wears a nappy to bed I don't know, but that's what he likes to hear. Then once snuggled into bed I have to encourage her to masturbate by saying, "That's it, baby, and cream for mummy. come in your nappy for mummy. Good girl, good girl. That's it masturbate for mummy, fill your nappy, darling."

"Ooh, I'm coming, mummy, I'm coming." And so he would. Nappy filled and all was right with the world. "Night, night, mummy." It might be all right with the world, but he was definitely not right in the head!

Some callers like to pretend they are dirty little sluts. They wear short dresses, stockings and suspenders, skimpy panties. Talk about how they would love to suck my boyfriend's cock.

"Do you have a boyfriend?" They sometimes enquire. When I give them an affirmative, you can hear the excitement in their voice. "Oooh," they follow this up with. "Does he have a big cock, does he loved being sucked?"

I laugh to myself and think, yeah, but not by some weird cock sucker like you, mate. But you have to say what they want to hear; after all it's what they are paying for.

One guy who I used to get quite often, was into me taking to a lingerie shop as part of his fantasy. I used to have to describe in great detail all the garments we'd find there. Sometimes we used to visit Anne Summers, but more often than not it was a regular department store. We'd decide on a few of the items I'd want to try on then I'd have to surprise him by selecting some for him to try on. We'd go into the changing room together, where he would assist me into some of the garments, caressing different parts of my body at the same time. I would take out the items I'd chosen for him and make him put them under great protest on his behalf, then shock him further by calling for the young Saturday girl assistant to help us by selecting different sizes. Anyway, in she bustled into the changing booth only to be stunned to find a man in there with me. I'd drag her in by her collar and I would proceed to seduce her. And, basically, that was his fantasy. He often used to ask if I would meet up with him and take him shopping. Always promised I might do one day, never intending to, but it keeps them interested and coming back. I know what you're thinking, it's wrong to lead them on. But really, that's what they want. So, it might as well be me doing the leading.

By day he was an ordinary bloke with an ordinary life. By night he was a greasy biker with a beard and a beer belly. However, he was no ordinary biker. He was a cross-dressing biker who, on occasion, wore a pink frilly tutu.

Whenever you get a new caller come through you can't help wondering what their particular peculiarities are. They nearly always feel the need to tell you what they look like. Sometimes, as with this guy, you wish they hadn't. You get a vision in your head and no matter how hard you try, that vision floods your mind every time they call you. He'd book a thirty minute call with me. I had him quite regularly; I was working for another company at that time. For the most part we used to chat. He'd start by telling me what he looked like. Beard, beer belly, hairy chest, short and fat, slightly balding. He managed a bathroom and kitchen centre in Sheffield. Really, a nice bloke, very chatty, told me all about himself and his personal life. And, he was what he said, an ordinary guy with an ordinary interest in ladies clothes.

I have to say, thanks to his detailed description of himself that the image of him sitting in his arm chair, puffing on his pipe, a short fat and balding man with a hairy chest on display while wearing his treasured frilly pink tutu will stay with me until the day I die!

114

So you see there are all kinds of fantasies. Real life ones, the ones they can't seem to get off their minds and have a strong compulsion to live out over and over again. Or, some have completely imagined ones too wild even for them to perform in real life. Others, want to be as totally outrageous as the chat lines will allow them to be without harming anyone, themselves included. But most I find just want a bit of dirty naughty fun.

A lot of it is born out of curiosity. Some don't even want to live out their fantasies it's for their minds only. Occasionally, it's some lonely guy who needs someone to talk to. Whatever their reason or need. I know I'm here for them. At a price? Well, obviously.

Chapter Ten

A Shoulder To Cry On

Hard to believe, I know, but sometimes we are looked upon as agony aunts or even expected to give out advice. One guy that springs to mind came through late one night when I was with premium rate lines. At first, he was amazed I was a real person. He thought he'd found a recorded story line.

"Hello, Jolene speaking..." My groggy voice greeted him. Well, I was asleep, which is natural at three in the morning.

"Oh, I didn't expect anyone to be there. I thought I'd got a recorded message."

"I can assure you, I'm not. I'm really real."

"Oh, sorry, I didn't mean to disturb you, I thought it was a recording I was going to be listening to."

"It's okay, that's what I'm here for, to chat."

"No, I'll go. I just wanted to listen to someone talking dirty."

"Well, you can, that's me. It's what I do for a living, you know." Even half asleep I could tell from his voice there was something amiss.

I know for a fact, from some of the guys I've spoken to on the PRLs, that most of the other girls doing the chat lines wouldn't talk about anything but sex. Which always amazed me, I mean you still get paid, no matter what. Me, I'm happy to talk about anything. Yes, I love the sex chat. But it didn't bother me either way what they spoke about. For the most part, with PRLs a lot of lonely guys would ring the chat lines, after all that's what we were to them, someone to chat to. Some used to say, it's nice to hear a woman's voice at the end of the day. Some would tell you their life story. They all said the same when they came through to me; that they'd listened to the messages and liked the sound of my voice. I listened to some of the messages, at the beginning, just to get some idea of what to say. Most of them were blonde, a few brunettes, but not one was a red-head. I wanted to be different. So I used the 'Jolene' in the Dolly Parton song. Sometimes wish I hadn't. The amount of callers who'd come through singing, ''Jolene'. This one time there was a whole gang of lads came on singing it. They were on speaker phone, they said. They were all laughing at the end of the rendition and so was I. It's funny, though. All my life people told me have their troubles. At the age of sixteen it started, perhaps I'm a good listener. Of course, when I became a barmaid I was in the perfect place for that job, too. So when guys came through just to talk, I'd just listen. And, I guess, that's what must have happened with this guy. He must have felt subconsciously, I was someone he could talk to. Now, back to him.

Silence over the phone prompted me to ask, "What's the matter?"

"I still can't get over the fact it's not a recording."

Smiling in the darkness of my bedroom, my voice softened.

"I can quite assure you I'm no recording."

"I know that. It's just..."

"We don't have to do the sex chat, if you don't want to. We can just talk."

He hesitated for a moment, contemplating my offer. "Yes, all right, I'd like that."

"Are you married?" I started with this, sometimes it could be they've just separated, or worst still bereft.

"No, never been married."

"What, not even a girlfriend?" I could tell by his voice he was no spring chicken.

"Oh, yes. I was engaged, once. Due to marry."

Now, it started to make sense. He was lonely.

"Well, surely you're ready to start looking, again. How long ago was it?"

"Twenty years ago."

"Twenty years! And you've never been with anyone else?"

"Can't. Don't want to be hurt again."

It turned out; he'd lived alone all these twenty years. No family, no woman, nothing. I told him he couldn't let life pass him by, that he had to allow himself to live, again.

"I can't. I just can't seem to let anybody in."

"You've built a wall around yourself, haven't you? You have to knock the wall down, brick by brick. You must want to. That's why you're telling me. That means there's a chink in the armour. A sliver a light is shining through and that's why you're reaching out to someone." I know all I told him were old fashioned clichés. But sometimes you just need to hear the obvious from someone else. I could hear soft weeping on the other end of the line. He said, after a few minutes. "You're right; I haven't spoken to anyone about this in twenty years. It feels so good to get it off my chest."

"It's a start. Think about it. That's why you've kept it hidden, because you didn't want to face the hurt you felt. Instead of getting rid of the pain, you've harboured it and it's grown. Now you're facing it, by speaking about it. The pain should start to ease and you can allow yourself to heal."

"Is it that easy? Is it really that easy?"

"Of course it is you daft bastard!" Now, we were both laughing.

He thanked me over and over again. Said in all this time it was the first time he'd ever put into words how he felt. Couldn't understand why he wasn't getting over it.

He said, "I'm so glad you turned out to be real."

"Good!" I said. "So am I, now stop wasting my time and your money and get out there and find yourself a real woman!"

Don't get me wrong, he was one of a kind. No one else has ever been quite as down as he was. But I did get quite a few guys come though and tell my about their pending divorces, or separations, and bereavements. Sometimes my heart did ache for them; I've been there so I know what it's like. If you recall, this was how I met the lovely man in my life, now. Because of all the heartache he'd recently suffered. Don't get me wrong that's not what he came through for, maybe none of them did until they heard my voice. He, like all the other guys who use the sex chat lines initially came through for a good old fashioned toss off! Until they realised they'd found someone to talk to.

I've had a few men come on the line, lonely in need of someone to chat to. I suppose it's the faceless voice. I think it's a sorry kind of world if we can't just talk, now and again. And, boy oh boy, do I like to talk!

Quite often they came through and just needed to know the particular fetish or fantasy was okay and normal. They just need a simple reassurance. Mind you, that being said, if you tell them you've heard a lot worse. They did sound a bit miffed, they like to think they're the only dirty bastards in the world and to anyone else they probably are! For some, there's a curiosity to the calls we get. Of course, they get off on that too. Dirty talk of any kind gets most blokes off.

I've even had guys through actually looking for advice on sex, women and our favourite positions and fantasies. On these lines we get it all. And a whole lot more besides.

One guy came through wanting a girl into corporal punishment. I gave him Simone, I like the sound of that name, gives an air of domination; it's a no nonsense sort of name. When I called him back he was looking for someone who was really into caning; a giver and receiver preferably. Naturally, he'd found the girl of his dreams. He wanted to know if I was really into S & M. Of course I was, had been all my life. Even to this day I visit S & M clubs. He wanted to know all the gory details, like how did I decide if I wanted to be the giver or the receiver. I told him I never knew until I started going through the procedure of getting ready to go to the club. Also my mood on that particular day would dictate my choice of garment. Apparently, he'd only had thoughts about it and wanted to speak to someone with experience as regards corporal punishment. We've never done the business, even after all this time; he hopes to one day meet me in real life where we can share our fetish with each other. I've advised him on joining a club himself, but he didn't want to go as a complete novice. So we both agreed the best thing for him to do was visit someone privately. Now, when he calls he fills me in with all the details and chats about his experiences with these women. Once a week or a fortnight he rings and this is what we chat about.

The best thing about it is, he does sounds a really nice guy and I do hope that one day he does find the perfect girl to share his 'interests' with. I'm sure he will do once he's brave enough to join his local S & M club.

He's been back again, Corporal punish man, as I now call him. I've been feeding him more lies. Sometimes you get into a thing without realising exactly what that involves. As I said earlier this guy wanted to chat to someone really into corporal punishment. I told him some cock and bull story about me being a member of and S&M club. Now he's come through wanting to know what I've been up to and has enquired as to when I next plan to visit the club. I'd forgotten

I'd mentioned to him the last time we spoke that I'd be going that following weekend. I told him I hadn't been and the poor chap sounded so disappointed. I felt I wanted to tell him something. I said the reason being, I was going to a hotel a few of the members go to which is owned by a couple who frequent our S&M club. We hired the entire hotel for four days and anything goes. Not everyone is invited just a select few. I added this just in case he wanted an invite. I do not know where I come up with such convincing rubbish! It's just there in my brain box. I've got a hidden talent for something, God knows what. Perhaps it comes from being an only child and I've always had to entertain myself. One thing's for sure it's very useful in this game.

Anyway, he seemed happy with the excuse, he hoped I'd have a good time and he would chat to me soon.

Low and behold, he came through yesterday wanting to know how I enjoyed my long weekend away. See what I mean about starting something...?

Had a wonderful time, I said. He wanted to know if I was submissive (caned) or dominating. Well, I gushed. Bear in mind this is all completely off the top of my head. I was sub, I told him. I was pushed into being a servant of the hotel's owners. She was my Mistress, bossy and cruel. He was the master who dished out the punishment.

Not a bad scheme, I told him, they had me as a free chambermaid for two days. But it was a fantastic weekend. You get to live out any fantasy and they are wonderful people. They hire the costumes and everything. I'm thinking as I'm writing this I wouldn't mind owning such a hotel. It would be brilliant. I'd be great at organising it and bringing peoples' fantasies to reality in a safe environment, obviously. No? Still just me and my imagination!

I know I've no real hands-on experience with most of the things we talk about on these phone lines, but I really believe I'd make an excellent sex therapist. I seem to have a natural affinity with just about any given subject, no matter how perverse. It's like second nature to me I know in an instant what the caller is really after.

Chapter Eleven

The Vicar And All His Wives

"Darling!"

Three years I've been doing the vicar and it always starts the same.

"Darling! Oh, darling. I've missed you so much, my baby. What are you wearing?"

"Aah, hello, Darling."

You just can't help it, every time he comes through you start saying it too. Darling! It, the word, and him drives you absolutely fucking stark staring bonkers! It wouldn't be so bad if he came through three or four times a week, but you get this about six to twelve times a day! Yes, a day! He runs up a bill of around fifteen hundred quid then you spend the next two months getting it out of him. It's only when I threaten him with paying him a visit does he cough up. He pays by cheque and I've always sent him an invoice. So, I know his address. Once he's paid, he's back again. So, there I am going through the performance yet again.

"I'm wearing black sheer silky stockings."

"Love you, darling. Go on, what else?"

You have to be slow with the description because he's seventy odd years old so you can't speak too quickly. Most

124

imes he's pissed as a fart. Plus, he keeps interrupting with his favourite word. "Darling!" And, everything must be black.

"A black suspender belt with a black satin thong that cuts right into my pussy lips."

"Oh, Darling! You dirty bitch. Oh darling, I miss you. When can we get married?"

This is his thing the whole time. He wants to marry the girl on the other end of the phone. We are in love and fate keeps us apart, therefore he's always ringing to persuade me, the girl, to marry him straight away. Apparently, I've to stop fucking around and get on with it! I wouldn't mind but I've been that girl about twenty different times and on three different companies! All these girls he has had me as have been spread over three years.

He tells you that he loves you, he wants you, and he needs you. I can't cope without you, darling. You're beautiful, you're gorgeous, and you're caring. Do you need a husband, I need a wife. When he's pissed it's the other way round. Do you want a wife, Darling. I need a husband. That's when I come off the fucking phone more confused than him!

You do want to get married don't you, darling? He's lonely, needs a woman in his life to take care of him. Then he finishes with, I can't cope, darling. I just can't cope. Your expected reply is, "I'll help you, darling. I'll care of everything."

"Will you, darling. Can I leave it all to you? Love you, darling. You're gorgeous. Aren't you, darling? Darling! Just say bloody yes."

"Yes!"

"Thank goodness for that. You do mess me about, don't you, darling."

Remember all the time I'm writing this and you're reading it. He's probably told me all this several dozen times in one night! This is because he has had me as so many different girls within my own company. I, unfortunately can't pass him on to another girl.

Including me as the owner, Chrissie. Me as my sister Sharon, she wrote to him telling him she's gone to work for a different company. I could have told him but the chances are he would have forgotten. So, I thought if I put it in a letter he'd remember the number. And, because he was a retired Reverend I told him the company was called 'Fallen Angels' and as I hoped, he fell for them. I was telling you about this in an earlier chapter this is how my new company name came about.

As I said he knows me as several dozen different girls, I thought it best to keep a little note or two on the whereabouts, ages, careers and family members and whether or not the girl in question was married, divorced, widowed or single. All this was very important to him. He loved looking on the map to see whereabouts you lived. Next time he rang you he'd tell you something about that area or a place close by.

One thing though, you could never be married or have a boyfriend. Because he is elderly, I decided to be a carer at a residential home, for one of his girls. Another I chose to be a midwife, because at one time he was a hospital Chaplain and one of his main jobs was to christen then bury still born babies. It goes without say it is the main reason why I put up with him. The thought of that poor man doing this awful task day in and day out. You couldn't help but feel for the man.

He's a very lonely man. He has two sisters, they are both married with children. Yes, I know he chose the life to live. But, what has been his reward? He's a lovely man to talk to, and you can do that sometimes, he tells you all about his life. Where he's lived and what it was like as a boy during the second world war. He was a man of the cloth through and through. Even in masturbation he had to be married. This is why he pretends you are his wife or at least wife to be.

During the throes of ecstasy he calls out, "I'm coming for my wife, my wife." Or if I do my fake orgasm bit, he still calls out, "Come for your husband, come for your husband. Ooh, darling. Did you enjoy that? You did didn't you, darling. You sexy bitch!" I love it when he says, "Talk dirty to me, darling. Make me come." He's so excited at the prospect of his 'wife' making him come, he doesn't always catch what you say.

"You're going to do what?" I can never tell if he's surprised or horrified. I chuckle away to myself and I have to repeat it without laughing. "You're going to what, darling. Piss on me? Oh I say, you fucking dirty bitch!" By now, I've collapsed into a heap. He has got such a posh well spoken manner and he speaks in his 'Reverend' tones. Sometimes I feel shocked at what I say. Then you hear him say.

"Come on, you bitch. Piss on my face. You fucking dirty whore!" Then I know we're off and running.

His favourite girl used to be Anna, she's thirty-eight, a blonde with big boobs and a shaven pussy. They all have to be of that description. Especially the shaven pussy and pussy rings or clitty rings. This is his biggest obsession, pussy rings and sex toys. He likes to get know everything about his latest 'would be' wife. Family, that's important to him. What she does for a living and where she lives. She lives in Blakeney and is the secretary of the local hotel. Actually, my best friend lives there and she was indeed a part time secretary at the hotel, but that was a long time ago. Secretary in a hotel is a responsible position and therefore the incumbent must have great organisation skills. He likes the woman in his life to take charge, as he puts it, and be able to organise him and our wedding arrangements. Then he talks about booking the church, and must have a honeymoon in Ireland.

The funny thing is once he's got this far, and the fantasy starts to become a reality, he changes to another girl. And, the merry-go-round begins again. The next time he came through wanting a girl who loves pussy rings. So I gave him Francesca, a lovely young sexy minx with five pussy rings.

Wish I'd known what I'd let myself in for when I came up with that story. Well, you just wouldn't believe. Anyway, it did the trick he's not changed from her in about three months. It's the longest I've ever known him stay with the same girl.

"Hello, is that Kev?" I know full well who it is, but I always somehow manage to pretend I'm not sure who the other person is on the phone.

"Darling!"

That dreaded word shrills down the phone. For some reason, known only to himself he always makes out you are the same girl he's spoken to with every company he uses. It's as though we are all one and the same. Except for Francesca, for some reason he's obsessed with the girl with five pussy rings. Read on all will become clear.

Because of his obsession with pussy rings I came up with the idea of telling him I had a girl with five pussy rings, seemed at the time quite innocent enough. Some girls do indeed have several pussy rings. Not with the Reverend, I'd forgotten the poor bastard had never even seen a pussy. The three days that followed of him talking with Francesca were unbelievable.

"I don't understand, Darling how can you have five pussy rings?"

So, for the umpteenth time I tried to explain again. "Two on the left, two on the right and the fifth one in the middle through my clitty."

"No, I'm sorry, Darling I'm just not getting it. Where, darling. Where?"

I'm thinking, fuck me you dozy old bastard what is there not to get!

Three days this went on for, I was nearly bald by the end of it. Of course what I hadn't realised at that time he's never seen a woman's fanny. He thought to have five pussy rings you needed five fucking pussy lips! Oh, my poor old Aunt Fanny.

Most often he comes on pissed as a fart, slurring. He can't remember his name, let alone the girl he's talking to. He'll say, "Come on, Darling. Don't fuck around. Why can't we get married? Just tell me." You start to do the chat then out of the blue, he'll say. "I've got to go, Darling. I just can't do it anymore." Twenty minutes later he's back again. The funniest thing is he'll always books a thirty minute call and he's nearly always gone in fifteen minutes or less. Sometimes he's been off the phone less than ten minutes, he'll say, "Can I book another call with you, darling." He's gone, then he's back ringing again to book another call. Another time you can't get rid of him. He'll say "I'll call you back."

You'll say, "Bye then, speak to you in a minute." All you get is, "But I love you, darling. I love you."

You chatter on saying, "Yes, yes, bye, bye." "Darling, Darling. I love you. For god's sake just say yes."

You say, "Yes darling."

He'll say, "Thank God for that. Christ, darling. You're hard work, aren't you? Aren't You!"

I must admit for the most part, when he's not driving you mad, he is quite humorous especially when he gets so frustrated with you, the girl, and the situation.

His latest girl at the moment is a black girl called, Molly. He came through one night asking if I had any black ladies working for me. I informed him I had indeed have a lovely lady called Molly. I used this name because I know for a fact that a previous company I worked for had a black girl called Molly working for them. Anyway it did the trick. Now we are off again, the hunt for his next wife. He is absolutely obsessed with Molly, thank God (and I do)! I told him I was from Alabama in the 'US of A' that's exactly what I said to him. Said I grew helping my momma to look after the little'uns when my papa passed away. Yes sir, I surely do. I's his black mamma and he's my white slave. He loves talking about putting his white man's cock into my beautiful black pussy all the live long day, my sweet honey chil'. Yes sir, I surely do. Yes indeed, my honey.

The first time I did this accent for Tom, he nearly pissed himself. Me, I still do! It's dreadful, I sound like someone from the deep dark south in the deep dark ages! I watched too many black and white movies as a child. That's my excuse and I'm sticking to it!

And on it goes, never fucking ending. It's like a mad carousel you can't get off. It's like being trapped in time. Lost in fucking space, more like. But, then, when he goes off your company and on to another. You actually miss the old twat! Even so, I'm glad he does, really. I'd probably end up slitting my wrists, or his throat! Still I can't complain, when he's on a roll you can earn up to two thousand pound a month out of him. Where does he get the money? God in heaven alone knows and thankfully, for the Reverend, He's not speaking. Couldn't get a bloody word in most likely!

Chapter Twelve

Bring On The Girls!

Now, this was a real test of my skills. These were all back when I was working on the PRLs. Girls phoning for sex chat. I know this contradicts all I said before about girls phoning chat lines. These however, were girls who were not the slightest bit interested in talking to boys. Once again, the men have been made redundant. Of course, I'm talking about lesbians.

I remember the first time I did a girl and told my good friend, Christine.

"Oh my God! What did you talk about?" she asked sounding absolutely horrified, at the prospect.

"Licking her pussy," I told her quite frankly. "That's what she wanted and that's what I gave her, a good licking out." It was beyond Christine's comprehension that I should want to talk to a girl and get her off. Then followed what always followed with Christine. "What did you talk about? What did you say to her? How did you feel about her saying the same things back to you?" As always, she wanted to know everything at once.

First and foremost, whoever or whatever you talk about it's only words. As far as me talking to another woman about having sex with her I simply imagined I was a woman asking a man to do things to my body. And, vice versa. I said I would do to her what I would want a man to do to me. It was that simple. Well, it must have worked. I brought this one woman off three times in the space of half an hour.

She was in her late twenties, married but she believed she had lesbian tendencies. She fantasised about having sex with a woman. Now, bear in mind, I have not nor will I ever be a lesbian. Well, not a true lesbian in the sense of the word. I did dabble a bit when I was fifteen. She was seventeen and the daughter of my mother's lodger's brother. I was still a virgin then and didn't know any better. Now, I like my cock too much, ask any guy. Nothing wrong with it, except I don't like pussy. I think they are ugly looking things, bit like a bloke with a limp dick. Certainly don't want one dangling in my face. Now, I'm not a prude if that floats your boat, well, that's great. I don't mind talking about it, as I've said before its only words. However, that being said. I was accused once of being a lesbian. I was twenty-two years old, separated from my first husband and, trying to better myself by attending adult training course. I'm usually pretty easy going, and get on well with both sexes. Always have done. Anyway, it seemed I was a bit too friendly for one of the women on the course; she spread it around that I was lesbian. There were four of us in this particular group, myself, Janice, Sue and this evil minded witch, Jackie. I think jealousy was at the root of the accusation. Mind you, I could be and still am, a little too friendly in the company of women. But, that's me. I've always flirted with men and women, alike. I'm not chasing either of them it's just a game I like to play. Thankfully now, all my girlfriends are okay with me and know I'm just larking around.

That being said, I have been misinterpreted since. My good friend Hannah, her sister-in-law thought I was one when she climbed into bed with me. Yes, she was still married to Hannah's brother. Did I mention he was laid on top of me at the time! Making fantasies come true for a living? I've done half of them in real life!

This past incident has come in handy in a way, like a few others I've encountered. Most guys come on and ask what I've been up to in my life and what turns me on. Well, for the most part this is how the chat begins. So, I do tell part of the truth some of the time.

Anyway, I digress. Getting back to this married woman who'd come through. She said she wasn't sure if she was a lesbian, but couldn't stop thinking about having sex with a woman. I told her that pretty much sounds like a lesbian to me. Anyway we got into the chat. I told her what I was going to do to her, undress her, slowly, kissing her from her neck down to her breasts. I would get her to squeeze my tits at the same time, then work my way down to her pussy, licking and kissing on the way. I told her how I'd pull her pussy lips apart and suck on her clitty like a nipple, suck it into my mouth then flick my tongue over it fast and hard. I told her

I'd use a vibrator on her. She said she had one there with her. So, I told to use it just as I told her to.

Three times I made her come, I was chuffed to bits with myself. I thought if I can convince a woman, I can convince anyone. I hadn't been doing the job long when she came through and she was my first woman caller.

I've had a couple more women through since her and one of them must have been the male equivalent in a lesbian couple because she did all the talking. I think she actually got off on the fact it was a straight woman she was talking to. I must confess she did actually turn me on. Well, I did cheat a bit. I imagined it was a man talking to me!

I've never had a girl come through on call backs, ever. We do get guys come through with their partner. Usually they want me to tell the girl what to do with the guy and his body parts. However, it's not very often we actually talk with the girl, they just listen to me. We sometimes do a two girl call with a woman from the same company. We talk as though we are in the same room and we have to say we are touching and licking each other and what we would do if the caller was with us. We all do that, all the companies, except little me. Well, I'm the only one at my company so I do them with myself. As I've said before, as long as I'm different ages I'm all right. Luckily, for me that's all they have been up to now.

Chapter Thirteen

Subs Doms And Humiliation

Domination and humiliation go hand in hand. Guys, who get off on domination, love to be humiliated at the same time. It comes in many forms but it all boils down to one and the same. However, that being said everybody's idea of domination and humiliation is completely different. Some humiliation can lead to sissification or womanisation. As can domination. It's whatever turns the caller on.

One of my regulars likes me to dominate him into wearing my daughter's school uniform, this fantasy contains all the above fetishes. I dominate him into dressing like my little girl, that's sissification, and because I've taken pictures of him in my daughter's school uniform therefore enabling me to blackmail and humiliate him by keeping him with us always dressed as a little girl whenever he's with us, no matter who comes to call on me. Although it could be argued that it's called forced feminisation. In actual fact forced feminisation is making a man dress as a woman as opposed to a little girl. We get lots of these; it's a very popular fantasy. Except for forced feminisation, they are still one and the same. Every time he comes through he always asks to speak to Auntie

DeeDee. He does everything his Auntie DeeDee tells him to do.

Although domination can lead to torture, toilet slavery, strangulation and suffocation, none of these lead to humiliation and feminisation.

One regular caller of mine wants me to take him swimming, tie weights to his ankles and hand-cuff him. One wall of the swimming pool bears a large clock with a second hand. We both know how long he can hold his breath, but I like to take it a step further. Keep him down that bit longer, all the while sucking on his cock mercilessly. Or he likes me to grind my pussy into his face, again while still under water, suffocating and drowning him at the same time. Delicious!

Every time I make him moan he loses some of his precious air. Finally, I let him up for air, just in time. Next time, I leave it almost too late, he passes out. By this time, in reality, he's shot his load, as I save him from drowning by giving him the kiss of life.

A particular favourite chat for domination and humiliation is toilet slavery. Some guys even want to be kept chained to the toilet and be made to lick mine and all my girlfriends' pissy fanny and shitty arse after we've used the bog!

Some dirty bastards like to go a bit further by having us piss and shit directly into their mouths! Yuk! Imagine, they'd want a snog after. Dirty fuckers! No wonder someone invented mouth wash I bet it was a bloke! Think on, the next time your man say his mouth tastes like shit, don't kiss him for a week, he might be telling the truth!

Submission is not quite as popular as domination, when a guy comes through asking for a submissive girl. I usually give him Sophie, Sarah or Eleanor. Any soft sounding name that springs to mind.

These guys like to think the girl is causing themselves pain at the request or demand. The more you squeal or cry out the better they like it. Some like the girl to enjoy the pain, the more pain the bigger the turn on. The odd few like to think you don't enjoy the pain at all and actually want to hear you cry. That's okay by me, I can sob my little heart out for twenty-eight quid a time. Last week I got paid ninety-four quid for two guys to torture me over the phone. Oooh, I screamed like a banshee!

Some domination can be quite ruthless. Especially when they are doing the dominating. They want it to be very violent. I had this one regular with another company, evil bastard. Thankfully I've only had him a few times. Anyway, he came on the line booked a thirty minute call and for the most part he did all the talking. How he'd start was this; he was the king of his kingdom. Everyone in his kingdom did exactly as he said; he was very specific in his fantasy. Apparently, I was in a highly respected position, I was his personal assistant. However, he was interviewing my replacement which I had to sit in on because I was the one who had to test her loyalty. He even said what I'd be wearing, a lime green all in one cat suit. I had long brown hair with big tits. The zip on my cat suit was pulled down low enough to reveal all my tits without them actually hanging out.

The girl trying out for my position is blonde with huge tits, slim, beautiful and twenty two. First, I have to get out her tits and nail them to the dinner table. We are interviewing her in one of his restaurants. Of course, his entire kingdom is there to witness the testing of his new assistant.

"Go on," he orders. "Hold the fucking bitch still." Anyway this done, nipples nailed to the table. He then tells me to yank up her tits and rip her nipples off." Naturally, she's resisting. Well, who wouldn't! "Make the fucking bitch do it, go on hold her down. Put your fucking knee in the bitch's back." The waiter would appear with the starters of our meal. Yeah, right as if you'd have the stomach to eat anything! Especially not these hors d'oeuvres! Little morsels of dog shit, which thankfully only she has to eat. Of course she refuses, so he orders me to force them down her throat! She starts to cry and I have to smack her about. Then, he tells me to get everyone in the restaurant to smack her about. Each order he gives becomes more and more violent until the poor bitch is dead and I get to be his assistant a while longer. Lucky me! Thankfully, I've never had him through on my line and if I did, I would get rid of him! That's the beauty of your own company you can choose who to keep as a regular.

For the most part, none of them is quite as violent as this, usually, it's body worship and making them do things they don't want to do, which of course in reality they do. Like being made to lick your pussy, some guys prefer the word, cunt. I personally don't mind the word, but I think for the purpose of this book the word could become a bit overwhelming.

Domination is usually boot licking, or stocking leg shagging or using a strap-on on them. They do like a lot of that. Talking about spreading their butt cheeks and giving them a full length of my strap-on cock, it really does it for them; it does a lot for me as well! Ooh, I do it with such glee and full of meaning. I'd love to shove it right up their backsides!

They love the thought of being whipped, while they're getting shafted. For some, it's the sound of a thrashing that turns them on. This one caller kept shouting harder, harder. I was supposed to be thrashing his arse with a cane. I actually broke a wooden coat hanger, one night, whipping it against the seat of a leather chair for the sound effects. Even woke poor old Tom and nothing wakes him. Not even me in the throes of a fake orgasm when I'm laid beside him doing a call. Come to that, not even a real one wakes him!

Others like you to treat them like dirty bitches, sluts or whores and make them fuck themselves with a dildo or a bully boy (black, fist shaped dildo). You have to scream at them saying; "Spank your arse!" or, "Pinch your nipples!" "Slap your cock, pull your balls!"

You have to tell them you're going to make them take twenty or more cocks up the tight pink holes. Suck every cock dry. All the time you're whipping them into a frenzy!

After which, they thank me for a good time. To which I always reply, "You're welcome call anytime!"

Gleefully, I run downstairs to Tom. Who turns to look at me entering the sitting room, seeing a big beaming smile across my face.

"My God! Who were you trying to kill, up there?"

"Just some old pervert," I inform him quite blasé. "Boy oh boy do I love punishing them disgusting old or young perverts! I did enjoy that."

Domination comes in all forms; take this particular caller who's recently joined my stable. That's what Tom calls it.

I had a new caller through recently wanting to talk about his small cock. He was obsessed with wanking it. Anyway, as we talked, he confided that he often called out his wife's friends' names as he came. He continued by telling me more of his dirty secret desires, that's what he liked to call them. One of which was wanking in Pauline's bathroom, and he was contemplating going to her house with his wife in the near future. She was his favourite of his wife's friends. So, I started to talk about this proposed visit and what I wanted him to do. He got most excited at the prospect and encouraged me to tell him what to do there. I came up with this bizarre request. I wanted him to go to Pauline's bathroom and masturbate with the door unlocked. After which, I wanted him to leave a drip of spunk on the end of his cock and wipe it on the bar of soap on the bathroom basin. This suggestion filled him with pure delight.

Sorry guys and gals, but yes, I can be even more disgusting than them, you could say it goes with the job.

He had this thing about dark secrets and his telling me of them. One of which was his desire to see his wife with another man and how he wanted to be forced to lick this other man's spunk out of his wife's pussy.

He would spend the entire thirty minute call telling me all his dirty secrets. I was his confessor, you see. He told me how Pauline had stayed over the night before and how he had sneaked into her bedroom while she was out gallivanting with his wife. How he removed her dirty panties from her overnight bag and that he licked the crotch of her still-damp panties.

I said to him, why don't you wank into them?

"I wish I could, I'd really love to but I'm scared of being caught."

Another of my great suggestions surfaced. Then why don't you leave a smear of precome on them, it's clear and won't leave a stain. The thought of this excited him beyond believe. So much so, his time was up and he and he was about to come.

"Oohh," he groaned down the phone. "I need to book another call."

"That's okay," I said. "Ring the office."

He sounded so desperate on the phone I decided to let him suffer for a while and rang him back fifteen minutes later.

Grinning like a Cheshire cat, I said my apologies and hoped I didn't keep him waiting too long. To which he replied, "Can I tell you more of my dirty secrets?" Well, I was all agog!

This time his secrets were even dirtier. Lowest of the low, even by my standards. He told me how he often dress in his wife's panties and wore her lipstick. I asked what colour, knowing what the answer would be I just wanted to hear him say it. Red. Bright red. I had to stifle back a slight chuckle.

"And sometimes," he continued. "I like to walk and talk like a woman."

"Go on then," I encouraged. "Talk like a woman."

He faltered so I helped him along. "Say; ooh, I feel so horny!"

Well, the way he said it had me laughing out loud. I couldn't help myself. I made him say it again and he did. I rolled around my bed in fits of laughter.

You'd have thought it would have put him off, but it didn't. I asked him to put some lipstick on for me there and then.

"I can't," he replied. "My wife's back anytime. But I'll have some for next time."

"Okay," I said, "we'll keep it for next time. You know what this means, don't you? It means I'm one of your dirty secrets, now."

I never thought about it before but I guess in a way I'm most men's dirty little secret.

And, do you know what, I rather like the idea.

Just when I didn't think he could possibly get any more perverted, it did! Not only did he secretly go about wearing his wife's panties and lipstick, he searched out websites that contained big cocks. Especially big cocks for him to imagine sucking on. He apparently wanted his wife to bring a bloke back and be made to suck him off after he'd been inside her pussy.

I've had him a quite few times since. Apparently, he loves the idea of me being his dirty secret, of which he has many and takes great pleasure from telling me all about them in every gory little detail. I love the fact that he sees me as his dirty secret and I play on it every time he comes through. Last time he booked a thirty minute call I could hear is other phone ringing. It rang several times while we were doing the chat. I said, "Someone sounds keen to get through to you."

"Yes," he replied almost in a whisper. "It's the wife!"

Well, as you can imagine, I went into overload!

"Go on answer the phone, I want to hear you squirm knowing you've got your dirty secret on the other line." Of course, he didn't, I just like the reaction I stirred in him. I guess I'm just a wicked little girl at heart! Some might say an evil witch but I don't think I'm quite there, just yet!

The dirty bastard's only gone and done it! He's only gone and done what I told him to do. I didn't think he had the balls. He's only visited his wife's mate, Pauline and left a drip of spunk on her bar of soap in the bathroom!

He rang last week, they'd visited Pauline just before Christmas with her presents. He excused himself went up to the bathroom and did exactly what I told him to do. Now we've stepped over the mark, we've brought fantasy into reality. Something I thought I'd never do. Still I've said it before and I'll say it again, it takes all sorts to make a world and my world seems full of them!

Anyway, this is basically what domination is all about, it's many different things to many different guys. They either do the dominating or they are submissive or vice versa, a bit like this next guy I'm about to tell you about. He's into being beaten up by an Amazon-like woman. He likes to think of me as a lady wrestler and I actually have to talk about beating him up. All he says repeatedly is, "Can you pick me up and throw me over your shoulder?" I have to say I could pick him up and throw him on the bed, jump on him and suffocate him into submission. He's obsessed with a woman physically manhandling him. I'd be saying through gritted teeth, "Suffocate you bastard. Suffocate!" To the sound of him shooting his load. I don't have to tell you I said it with such gusto and conviction I really did want to suffocate the little weed!

There's actually a good few of this type of guy around who are into being bullied by their partner. I had one guy who used to ring on his mobile saying his wife had left him locked up in his bedroom and how he was terrified of her. How sometimes she goes away for a couple of days at a time leaving him locked in! Again, she's another one who would bring men home and have them fuck her in front of her husband. Sometimes he would cry down the phone and beg me to rescue him. He said I was the only one he could talk to and he tell me all sorts of rubbish about the things his wife did to him. Of course, it was all just fantasy, but this is what they get off on!

The strangest domination request I used to get regularly was a guy who wanted me to be really big; fat and tall. He wanted me to have long dirty finger nails and toe nails. I had to say, "I'm going to force my dirty long finger nails into your mouth and make him suck them."

He'd plead, "No! No, I don't want to, please don't make me!"

I had to laugh a lot at his helpless pleading, when squeezing him with my fat body. I had to have my girlfriend with me, a big black lady. I had to tie him to me, while she came up behind him and shafted him up the backside. I had to snog him and dribble spit into his mouth or sometimes I had to make him eat food he didn't like from my mouth. Tell you what, girls and boys, there's nowt as queer as folk!

Domination that leads to humiliation with a hint of blackmail, now that's very popular. I have several guys into this. It varies from having information on him which he has obviously given to me, accidentally on purpose, naturally. I would say I've set up a hidden camera in his flat and filmed him dressing in women's clothes, usually his sister's and tossing himself off furiously into a pair of her knickers. I tell him I shall send the video to his mother if he doesn't do as

I ask. One of his favourite punishments is making him suck his landlord off in front of the landlord's wife. Or I'll make him dress like a tart and bring men back to his flat and talk about him performing sexual acts with them. The amazing thing is he's a Geordie who lives in Germany, he works for a big car dealership out there. And, because he lives out there, I could charge him vast amounts of money for the pleasure of humiliating him and it was such a great pleasure too!

One young lad I used to get coming through quite a bit was into blackmail and humiliation. I convinced him so strongly about my intentions that I frightened him off completely. The last time I spoke to him he told me he'd moved and to ignore all the information I'd given him as it was no longer relevant. Can't handle the heat, stay off the chat lines is what I say. Needless to say, me and Tom peed ourselves over that unfortunate mortal.

Take this next guy; he wants me to kill six men, not just ordinary men either. They had to be six inch men. That's right; six inch men and I had to kill them with different parts of my body. Again, I had to almost kill them first, bring them back from the brink only to finish them off once and for all. One, I had to tread on, squeeze him with my toes. Another I had to roll on him, squashing him. Another one between my legs and I mean up my fanny, another one up my rear end. Finally, the last little man I had to place in a jar sit on it and fill it with shit. We never get to the sixth man he's usually cum by then. I mean, what's that all about, six inch men? Is he on a different planet or drugs or something!

Another time he came through and wanted me to torture and kill five old men in an old folks' home. I had to be a young trainee nurse, a sexy but evil teenage girl. I had to tie them to their beds with the promise of sexual favours. The first one I was to suffocate with my pussy. Slowly, naturally. Let him come back up for air, before killing him off completely. All the others were blindfolded so they didn't have a clue what was happening, to begin with.

The second, I had to put a plastic bag over his head and tighten the draw string around his throat. In his final gasps I was to rip a tiny hole where his mouth was and let him get his breath back only to snog him until he died with my mouth over his.

The third, I had to sit on his face with my arse over his mouth shit in it and squeeze my thighs together while he choked to death on it.

The fourth and final old bloke I had to drag to the bathroom and drown him in a bath full of water repeatedly letting him up for air before shoving him back under. There was a fifth but we never got to him because he came. He thanked me, and said, till next time.

Amazing what they think up in their lonely little rooms. I'm so glad I'm no longer in my lonely little room. I think I'd give up on men if it wasn't for Tom. He's just your normal average pervert!

Chapter Fourteen

Staying Power!

This chapter is about guys who have been with me since I first started doing call backs, over two years ago. The first one I'm going to tell you about is my absolute favourite caller of all. He's a gentleman, easy to do. For the most part, I enjoy getting him off, as I do with most of my callers. The only ones I don't enjoy are the ones who think once they've had you, they can call for any other reason except to book a call. But this is another chapter.

Yes, I actually enjoy getting them off. If I didn't, what would be the point? Money? Oh, yes, there's that, but unless you actually enjoy what you do you can't give the caller a good time and you certainly couldn't listen to them day in day out, night after night, week after week, for months and months on end.

So this chapter is dedicated to all my guys who have been with me since forever! You know who you are!

This first guy I want to tell you about actually lives not far from my home town, but of course he doesn't know it. Because of his accent, I felt as though I knew him from the first time he came on line. His fantasy is usually about his girlfriend and sometimes her daughter. No, not underage, she's seventeen. Mostly it seems she's quite a bit of a cow, the daughter. So, he gets off on hearing about nasty things being done to her and her mother, and especially teaching the daughter a lesson. He said to me one day, feeling a bit guilty. "You know, I wouldn't wish any harm on either of them and I'd be devastated if anything did happen to them. It's just that imagination is a wonderful thing. I like to fantasise about it happening to them knowing it's only ever in the realms of make believe."

I do him as Mary. From the first time he came through he's had me as her and he's never had me as anyone else.

I usually start by kidnapping him and his girlfriend. Me and my six big burly boys with large sexual appetites. They are always dressed in black, with black head masks so that all you can see is their eyes and, when called for, their cocks.

The twist is he's actually arranged for the kidnap to take place. We bundle them into the van where I have to tell her in great detail what's about to take place. Of course, she's horrified by this information and this is the turn on for him. That and him being tied to a tree while we, my boys and me prepare her for torture. It is true what he says, imagination is a wonderful things. We never seem to get any further than stripping his girlfriend very slowly, revealing parts of her anatomy, when it's all over but the shouting, moaning and groaning. Sometimes it's two old dears having a go at her. The thought of her being snogged by a couple of old dykes giving her a good gumming round both sets of lips drives him into a frenzy!

As I said, sometimes it's the daughter, sometimes both. For some reason we never get further than them being stripped. It seems to be my description of what's about to take place that turns him on, and gets him off! Don't get me wrong we never torture the mother and daughter together. And, he's never the one doing the torturing; he leaves that in my very capable hands. Another variation is his girlfriend's mother and father doing unspeakable things to her that's another turn on for him. Whatever his little heart desires I just love to perform.

Sometimes I'm in this fantasy; his girlfriend is off visiting her parents but he's suspicious. He's 'called me' to go with him to spy on them. I have to take a sneak peek through the window where, of course, I catch the three of them at it and I have to tell him in every gory detail, slowly revealing to him what the three are up to.

He sounds so much like he's having a real dirty good time on the other end of the phone, I really do enjoy getting him off!

Another guy who's been coming back to me from the beginning, along with several other companies has had me under several guises, and again the fantasy is always the same and amazingly it has been for the last three years. I'm always his wife, who's parted from him and I have to torment him with all the other men I've been sleeping with, from his best friends to his brother, father and grandfather. Of course, they are all better at it than him.

It always starts the same, he misses me and loves me with all his heart and even though I'm a shameless hussy for sleeping around, he's prepared to forgive me. Then I have to go into gory detail of who I've had since last we spoke and more importantly, how big they were.

"I'm lost without you. When are you coming home, babe. I miss you desperately."

"I'm not sure it's a good idea. You never believe me when I tell you I've been faithful."

This is how we always begin, he mistrusts me. Thinks I've been shagging around behind his back all the time, which of course I have. That's the whole point of the fantasy.

"Please, babe," he continues to beg. "I can't sleep without you by my side. I'm so lonely without you." Then we start a bit of a nicey nicey lovey dovey chat. Then he asks who I've seen. Then the accusations start to fly, and then he wants the gory details of who, where and how often. I have to tell him the size of cock I've taken, how it filled me up and stretched me to capacity, how I couldn't get enough of it and would beg him to do it again, the positions we did it in. The worse I made it the better it got for him. Ooh, and how I just love whipping him into a frenzy. Maybe that's why he comes back time and again.

As I say, this is how the fantasy goes. He mistrusts me, accusing me of shagging everyone who comes in contact with me but he'll forgive me if I admit I've been shagging all the blokes he's been accusing me of. I leave him saying I'm innocent. Then the final twist comes when I tell him he was right all along. He forgives me and takes me back, then the next time he comes through. It's because I've been shagging around. Again.

Another guy I've been having through all the companies is a black guy. I would say from his accent, he's Jamaican. He's my black slave and I'm his white mistress. Again, it's a play on words, I have to keep talking about my white pussy and his black cock. I've been doing him for nigh on two years now and it's always the same. He's made to lick my white pussy and I want his big black cock stretching my white pussy lips and tell him how he's a slave to my white pussy. For some reason, he never lasts for very long. He's my black slave and I'm his young white mistress.

It's not just my white pussy he wants to lick clean but also drink a white man's come out of me. He wants me and my boyfriend to both use him for our sexual gratification. His two favourite words whatever we talk about are black and white.

I actually spoke with a black girlfriend of mine and asked what would be the best chat for him and she told me to speak of my wet glistening pink folds. Apparently, this really gets black guys off and she was right, it did!

Another regular wants me and my sixteen year old daughter together. The fantasy is he's my eighteen year old daughter's boyfriend who just happens to have the hots for the mother. We do every scenario imaginable. Sometimes he has the daughter first, then me, or the other way round. Then we surprise him by the two of us pouncing on him together.

This is quite a popular fantasy, mother and daughter. As is wife and mother-in-law. But that's another chapter.

I have countless guys coming through who I've had from day one. Another such caller is an absolute gentleman; we do get them from time to time. He's into long legged girls who wear sexy underwear. He's calling round to see me on some pretence. And, I have to be wearing a silky robe which falls open to reveal stockings, suspenders and lacy bra. Unable to resist, he takes me on the dining room table, or over the back of settee, up against the wall in the sitting room and occasionally, in mine and my husband's big bed. As with a lot of blokes it's the stockings and suspenders that do it every time. They love the feel of the stocking brushing against their skin. Maybe that's why so many of my callers like wearing them! He's just an everyday guy with every day fantasies.

Another firm favourite of mine is a guy whose fantasies are simple and mainstream. He's either the television repair man or the gardener or post man. Once he was even a chimney sweep, then a builder. The fantasy; he's a dirty workman and I'm a rich, posh bitch desperate for a big dirty cock. I offer him payment in kind because I've no money to pay for the work he's just carried out, but then at first, he refuses. Then I have to throw myself at him begging him and teasing him until he gives in. Then when he's about to give it to me I change my mind whereupon he makes the spoilt bitch take it good and hard.

Phew! I like this fantasy. It's never boring, he's got a good imagination, plus I like doing the things he does.

Most guys call through about once or twice a month. Some, as often as once or twice a week. However, some guys come through every other night, but these are few and far between. One such caller springs to mind. I don't get him anymore; he's the one who still owes me a large sum of money. When I did used have him coming through just about night after night, it was over a period three months.

It was always the same. He was allegedly separated from his wife, but still lived with her because he had nowhere else to go. This in itself I found a bit odd. I know I'm fond of saying, it takes all sorts, but this really did.

Anyway, the thing was he's downstairs sleeping on the settee while his wife is asleep upstairs. He would chat to me as Dee, getting to know me as he thought, while doing the chat. Sometimes we had to be quiet as he could hear his ex-wife wander about in her bedroom. We would chat sometimes for an hour or two, and then he'd decide to go up to where his wife was sleeping. He told me he still fancied his wife and wanted to touch her while she slept, because, of course she wouldn't let him anywhere near her awake.

Over the weeks, he told me all the details about why they'd split up and how he couldn't afford to move out, blah, blah, blah.

Anyhow, when he was stood at his wife's side, he'd ring me back and tell me where he was and what he was doing to her. At first, I went along with him. Told him what to do to her and all that shit! However, the things I had him doing including taking her pants off and licking her pussy, which to be honest when I heard him smacking his lips I really started to believe he might be doing. Then I told him to pull her lips open and finger her then rub his cock over her clit and slip it into her pussy. Or I'd get him to rub his cock over her face and push it between her lips and spunk over her. All the time it would be in hushed tones and he would tell me back what he was doing. Well, all I can say is, she must have been a heavy sleeper or at some point before he rang me, he must have drugged her. This went on for weeks, almost night after night and amazingly, she never woke once!

Occasionally, it would be his wife's sister over for the weekend. Where was she sleeping on the sofa opposite him! Of course then the whole charade would start again, this time with her.

In the space of two months he must have spent around two thousand pounds in phone calls. And he still managed to leave me, owing me six hundred quid, or thereabouts. I don't know, maybe I got greedy. I should never have allowed him to get so high. Whatever the reason, I never wanted anyone who used me and my company to ever get into so much debt. So, I said thank you, and goodbye. I'd made a tidy sum out of the guy. He has been though once since wanting another call. Although I'd written his debt off, I wouldn't give him another one but just chatted with him for a while for old time sake just to see how he was getting on. He had finally moved out of his wife's house. And now, instead of working for himself was now fully employed, still trying to pay his debts off. I told him not to worry about paying me, but at the same time it would be the last time I spoke to him. I wasn't being funny; it's just that I only give up my precious time to paying callers. The rest of my time is booked with my lovely man, Tom.

Another guy I get most weeks since time began is a very sexy Scottish gentleman. He's always had Yvonne, a sixty-six year old. He likes the older woman and has done since he and his girlfriend were seduced by an older lady when they were in their twenties. When I gave him Yvonne's description it reminded him of his old landlady of thirty odd years ago.

Apparently, she was their landlady in her late fifties. He was living with his girlfriend and the three of them were quite friendly. Especially, her and his girlfriend. They even used to discuss his sexual attributes while he was out. Anyway this one particular afternoon, he'd got off work early and planned to do some daytime entertainment of his own and treat his girlfriend to some afternoon delight. So, there they were in the bedroom, her on the bed, him stood at the foot of it. Her legs were resting against his body, feet each side of his head as he gave her a good slow seeing to. Unbeknown to them the landlady was stood watching them in the bedroom door way. It was only when she entered the room that they noticed her. He told me they were too far into the shagging to protest and besides his girlfriend encouraged her to come in. She stood beside them saying, "That's it. Don't stop. Let me watch your cock stretch her pussy." Of course this turned him on so much it reflected in his love making with his girlfriend, which she enjoyed immensely. Now he could feel the landlady's hand massaging his arse and balls. Feel her big saggy tits (his words) rubbing against his back. Then she reached down and started to grope his girlfriend's tits and rub her clit.

Well, as you can imagine it didn't take too long for them to come. They enjoyed a couple more threesome sessions over the following weeks and a few times his girlfriend gave him permission to shag the landlady on his own. Naturally, life takes over and eventually they all went their separate ways and so, to this day, he still talks about it and it still makes him rock hard. He's in his fifties, now and it still turns him on like nothing else.

This last guy I've had almost since I began running my own business, is a particular perverted creature. He always asks for a dirty old bitch. Usually he has a twenty minute mobile costing him twenty-eight quid. He has two or three of these a night every other month.

The description is always the same she has to be a dirty old slapper who's in a short skirt with her big tits hanging out. The things she has to get up to is nobody's business. I think I've done everything from shagging my boyfriend's father to letting a dog lick me out!

He is by far and away one of the dirtiest callers I've ever encountered!

To me though, he's one of the most entertaining guys I do on a regular basis. I love it, you should know by now I'm a kinky, dirty bitch who just loves turning all the men on and helping them to fulfil their darkest desires!

Chapter Fifteen

Cock And Ball Torture

The words conjure up all sorts of terrors for some men. I know it does for Tom. Most calls I can tell him about, but these calls make his balls creep up inside him. You know what I mean, don't you boys? Unless of course, this turns you on!

It is the one subject I dreaded.

A, because I was crap at it and;

B, I couldn't bear the thought of causing anyone pain. I used to hate it when the reception called and said it was domination. Usually, that meant cock and ball torture. However, all that was about to change.

He was a regular with the first company I worked for. He had tried most of her girls, but for some reason he would go off the girl he spoke to. He was a good caller, came through once or twice a week for up to two hours. So, the money was good.

Anyway, the owner of the company came through and told me all about him; what he liked to talk about and especially, what not to talk about. And, what I had to bear in mind that whatever I told him to do he would carry out. Yes, you'd be surprised how many guys will actually do what you tell them to do.

So, I had to ring him and do the chat. He seemed a nice bloke, he's from the north-east and a teacher. Or so he says, remember the callers, like the chat girls don't always tell the truth about themselves. From what I could gather, he liked to be controlled by women and for some reason young girls from thirteen upwards. When I say controlled I mean just that. If the young girl who I believe to be his niece said he had to sit in his house with no clothes on in the middle of winter, he would do it. And, he would. I had to ring him around eight one evening in December and every time he spoke his teeth chattered. I spoke to him like this for two hours. How does a thirteen year old get to do this to a grown man in his late thirties? That's easy, her mother, his sister has been controlling him like this all her life, and she got her daughter to start playing the game, too.

From what I could gather, from our chats he was obsessed with seeing young girls' knickers. Not touching, just looking. Apparently, it all started when he was really young. His sister had caught him looking at her knickers when he was about seven and her ten. She soon realised she could get him to do anything for a look at her knickers. That's when control took him over. Now, he's been like it all his life. He knows it's wrong, but it's completely out of his control. So, the reason he calls us is to punish him. And, punish him we do.

I personally had no idea how to 'punish' a man's cock, so who did I turn to? Yes, you've guessed it. Tom! I asked him what I could do to cause him some pain.

He said, "Tell the fucker to rub some deep heat into his knob, that'll sort him out." It sure did. That did the trick.

He, the caller, also gave me a few ideas, too. For example, getting him to tie things to his cock and balls. He said to me this one time that he'd got some string. I told him to fetch it, which he did. Then, I asked him what he had around the house. He said he'd got a statue close by, quite heavy. Tie that to it, then. He did as I said, then informed me he'd left the string too long, the statue was laid on the floor. That's okay, I told him. Stand on a chair. He carried out my orders, and balanced on a chair. What he didn't expect, however, was that the statue was really too heavy for his cock and he lost his balance and fell off the chair. Well, there was such a clatter. Followed by the sound of something breaking. I think he said it was a table lamp.

Well, when I finished the call I ran down the stairs to tell Tom all about what had happened on the call. He shook his head in total disbelief. "And, he actually did it? He actually did what you told him to do?"

"Yes, babe. But, that's not the best. He lost his balance and fell off the fucking chair and smashed a table lamp." We absolutely pissed ourselves laughing. And, I said, "isn't this the best job ever!" We just couldn't stop laughing.

Anyway, he came through the next week. This time I got him to tie a tin of spaghetti hoops to his cock and to make sure the string left the can about two or three inches off the floor, then I told him to walk up the stairs. I swear to God you could hear the tin clattering on the stairs and I could hear him moaning and groaning with pain with each knock of the can. As you can imagine me and Tom were in fits later on. We kept thinking up of all these things we could do to him. He said to me, "Tell him to shut his ballocks in a drawer!" So, I did!

Next time, I did as Tom suggested. I got him to go into his office. He was always naked, by the way when I rang. Told him to stand at his desk, pull the drawer out, place his balls inside and slam the drawer shut. But, I didn't quite feel that was enough even though the poor bastard was bawling his eyes out! I still needed to punish his cock, after all that was the main offender. So, I asked him to find the heaviest book. He told me it was an encyclopedia. I ordered him to pick it up and hold it at arms' length. I left him standing there while I went down to tell Tom what I was doing to him. "And, Tom, He actually cried when I told him to slam the drawer."

"Serves the fucker right!" He had no sympathy for the guy. "You haven't left him standing there?"

"Of course, it's all part of being in controlled; he loves being told what to do." I left him there for ten minutes. I would have left him a bit longer but Tom was going on and on. He wasn't concerned for the guy left standing there; he was more concerned he wouldn't be calling me back!

Anyway, when I went back upstairs to finish the punishment, he was still standing there and from the sound of the straining he was doing holding on to the book for so long, he wouldn't have been able to do it for much longer. There was a brief sound of relief as he let go of the book followed by an anguished cry of pain as the spine of the book fell on his cock. Can you believe, an erect cock!

Now, I was beginning to get the hang of cock and ball torture. I was beginning to enjoy myself. Starting to get really adventurous. Really getting into the swing of things, quite literally, as it goes. We were starting to get a bit more risky. I wanted to show him off to the neighbours. One of the things I used to make him do was drive about with his cock out. Because it was one of the things his sister and niece used to make him do. They were never with him when I rang. She just used to phone him up. Told him to strip off, drive round to her house while she was out and make him do her housework. Good fucking scheme, if you ask me. I wished I lived a bit closer!

So, we'd done the riding around bingo halls and churches and through the town centre. I felt it was time to give the neighbours a treat. All the time I used to get him to walk or stand at the window, completely naked. I use to get this vision of him standing with his legs apart, his hands on his hips with some object hanging from his cock. I know, I know but that's how this job gets you. Maybe it was something to do with Robin Williams in that film, Hook which had something to do with it. Was it an image of Peter

Pan standing with his hands on his hips? Or was it the fact that this guy's name was Peter. I haven't got a clue, I just knew him emulating the Peter Pan stance with something swinging between his legs while completely naked made me collapse!

Anyhow, I told him this particular night we were going to give the neighbours a special treat. I told him to tie a can of hoops to his cock, short enough so it wouldn't catch on the ground. I wanted him to stand behind his front door, starkers in the dark. And, when I gave the command he was to open the front door. He said it was too dark for anyone to see him. I thought, they will in a minute! I want you to flick on the light switch, stand with your hands on his hips swaying to and fro two or three times before switching the light off. I just had this wicked vision of some poor bastard going by and catching a glimpse of this madman, then the front room light would go off and they wouldn't be sure if what they hd seen was real or imagined.

Well, as you can image, me and Tom, couldn't get over this for weeks. We pissed ourselves! He said "You fucking evil bitch! I'm glad I'm not on the bad side of you!"

Just remember the next time you see some poor bastard with his cock out, think on. He could be some daft twat just following orders!

That's the lighter side of cock and ball torture out of the way. Now, for the darker side of it. This next regular calls from France. His bag is more serious, ball cringing, you could say. Guys of a nervous nature skip this next part. I'm not exaggerating!

"Hello, mistress. First, I want you to tell me how you will prepare my body for your pleasure. You can take me to your dungeon or chambers to punish me. Do to me what you will. But I want you to finish by cutting the ball sac, releasing the balls. Torture the cock however you see fit. Then, I want you to castrate me on the final milking of the cock. If that's destroyed, I want you to take the cock, too."

Oh yes, this is the real McCoy. Before you read on, I want you to bear in mind that this was all of the top of my head. This was the first time I spoke to him, and, unbelievable as it may sound, each time he came through the description of what I did to his cock and balls got more and more severe.

"Right, slave. First of all, you will be stripped. Head mask on, hands tied behind your back. Leg clamps restrict your walking and for the most part you will be dragged through my dungeon and thrown before me. I will rip the mask from your head so you can see all my torture implements before you. You will be in no doubt at what's about to take place. You will be lifted and secured to my torture table. As you can see the table is in the shape of an upside down 'Y'. Your legs will be spread wide to allow easy access to your cock and balls. Your hands and feet will be manacled to the table and a neck brace will keep your head perfectly still. As you will see, there is a mirrored ceiling. I don't want you to miss seeing one single act of punishment that's about to take place. Now, my servants will attach clamps to your nipples and scrotum. These will have weights hanging from them and they will be added to as we progress. Your foreskin will be pulled back and stinging nettles will be wrapped around your bell-end. I will drip candle wax down your jap's eye, until the tube is filled and it will be left to harden. In the meantime I will cut the ball sac in readiness for castration."

All this is said in a cold, deliberate, calculating voice, because I had to think quickly before I told him every step of the way what I was about to do to him. I had to take my time over each course of action. Of course, every time I fed him more information. I heard in groan in horror at what I was about to do.

"Now, the wax has hardened I'm going to take up my metal meat tenderiser and smash hard against the shaft of your cock shattering the wax inside the tube, so that on the final milking your spunk will shoot out through the shards of wax making your final orgasm excruciatingly painful. And, now, I'm picking up the castrating shears with my left hand and on my right hand you will see I'm wearing my milking glove and if you look carefully you can see it's peppered with tiny dots of steel spikes. So, as I give the cock its final milking your foreskin will be in tatters and the cock will have to be destroyed. And I will take the cock with the balls. I'm starting the final milking of the cock, the shears are in place and I'm ready to cut the cords. Can you feel the tiny spikes slicing into your cock?"

"Aaahhghh. Yes, Mistress. I'm ready for the final milking"

"Are you ready to shoot, and feel the wax shards down your shaft."

As he comes I tell him that I'm cutting the cords, as he's finishes spurting I say, I've picked up the machete and am slicing off the cock."

Horrific, isn't it? Still it's all in a day work! And, it does beat working for a living.

I have a young caller who comes through a couple of times a month, always asks for a cheeky girl. God knows why, it's more than a cheeky girl he's after it's more like a psychotic bitch!

The fantasy is; a girl in her early teens and she's out with several of her mates on the piss who comes across this youth minding his own business when he's set upon this group of girls. They start off by bad mouthing him, swearing and spitting on him. The girls follow this up by dragging him by his hair out of the bus shelter and start to kick him in the balls and stamp on his cock. Then, they rub their arses into his face, then piss on him. Till finally they all kick and punch the fuck out of him. To which I hear him groan as he obviously shoots his load.

He thanks me for the call and hopes I enjoy the rest of the evening and bids me good night. Oh, it's not uncommon, most of the guys I talk to often end the call in a similar vein.

I've done this for over three years now so nothing surprises me anymore. Well, that's not strictly true. I must just tell you this, this is totally unbelievable. This guy rang looking for a mistress specialising in cock and ball torture. So, I gave him the woman I gave all my Dom and torture calls to, I gave him Simone. Surprisingly enough he wasn't looking for someone to chat to about it. He was actually looking for someone to perform the acts we spoke of and that was ball destruction. He informed Simone, of a mistress he used to visit who destroyed one of his testicles and now he was looking for one to destroy the other. He even told me in great detail how she went about doing it. To cut it short, she stamped on it smashing it, he even told me the noise it made, 'Pop!'. I do so hope it was all part of the fantasy. I'm very pleased to say he is not one of my regulars, I've only had him twice. Unlike most calls that I do, I do the best call I can so they come back. On this occasion, just like a few others I didn't want to come back. I gave him a shit call.

Hopefully, he's found someone to do the job, I hate the thought of him haunting any other poor bitch on the phone!

However, the man who inspired me the most was an elderly gentleman called Alan. He is 76 years old and is into torturing women, especially women with plenty of meat on their bones. His two most favourite women to torture were Britney Spears and Kelly Brook but, with a slight twist (as if he wasn't twisted enough!) He wanted to be Britney Spears and I had to torture him, as she. I on the other hand when it was my turn had to be tortured had to be Kelly Brook. Why these two particular girls? Well, as I said he liked women with fleshy breasts and thighs and these two seem to feature on a daily basis in the national newspapers usually clad in minute bikinis . He absolutely delighted in slicing off Kelly's breasts and thighs, especially to the sound of my piercing, shrill screams. The more agonised I sounded the more he delighted. I know a few will think I've encouraged this barbaric behaviour but he was a lovely old chap to talk to and very polite.

We often had a little chat or a chuckle before our torture began. I did him as 22 year old Debbie. He tried a few of my other girls but for some reason he favoured Debbie. Maybe it's because I/she would do it with such glee and enthusiasm. Sometimes he would wear his torture bra all day in readiness for me to torture him as Britney. He designed the garment himself, he told me, fashioned it from a strip of linoleum. He draped it around his neck the two end strips hung down passed his nipples and were secured to his chest with a belt. He then drew pencil marks where his nipples sat pressed beneath the linoleum then proceeded to push and twist a couple of screws through the material so that he could slowly screw them into his nipples giving them a twist and a turn whenever his desire willed him. The flashes of pain would throb through his torso right down to his cock.

Occasionally, he would tell me about some medieval torture performed on women he'd read about recently in the library. Or sometimes it was torture performed by the Nazis on women during the war. He was almost gleeful and manic in his retelling of the suffering bestowed upon the female form. Once we'd talked about the torture and what the poor woman must have been going through we would re-enact it through Britney and Kelly. It wasn't something he wanted to do for real, he simply wanted to imagine and try to experience the pain for himself, as a woman. This was his turn on.

And its thanks mainly to him; I've become so good at verbally torturing men over the phone.

Mr P was not the only guy I spoke to who was turned on by the thought of him being abused as a woman. I had this one regular who still comes through now and again, he too wanted to be a young woman sexually abused by men. Usually, forced to suck cock. He, a young 12 year old virgin and the man abusing him was usually an authority figure, like a headmaster. He even went as far as dressing in a schoolgirl uniform and wearing a blonde plaited wig.

Sometimes, I'd be a schoolgirl with him being abused or we would merely get the teacher's cock hard. It was the thought of the older man so turned on by the young girl that he could not resist fucking the virgin schoolgirl's little tight pussy.

I think it's a lot to do with the fact that virgins are becoming younger and younger that does it for men. They love the thought of tight virgin pussies, either that or a tight arse. I truly believe that's how arse fucking came about, it's a nice tight hole to shove their cocks into and let's face it for most men that's what it's all about - shoving their cock into a tight hole, whether it's male of female or animal they don't give a fig as long as it's tight. Mind you, if their cocks were a bit bigger they wouldn't need such a tight hole to fuck!

Chapter Sixteen

Blackmail, Bribery And Those Who Give It Away

Amazingly, these guys actually ring through to book a call but when the girl rings them, no one takes the call. And they never ring to ask where the call is or why they were not around to take the call. Apparently, there are guys out there who get a kick out of paying for a call and not taking them. Mental!

I never actually believed it myself, at first. A few times when I worked with the other companies, I was told to ring a number, tried several times but to no avail. Just put it down to a change of mind, or sometimes what can often happens is a guy will book a call, it's taken longer than normal for the girl to get through and he's had someone turn up unexpectedly. He knows who's calling him and is too embarrassed to answer the phone. Since working for myself I have had a few calls where guys have booked and paid for a call, it's gone through on my card machine. But he's not there to take the call. And they never ring back. Unless, of course, it's to book another call.

Over the last few months I've been pestered by this one particular guy. At first he seemed your average Joe, nothing out of the ordinary, except he was a bit chatty. Some of them are. Didn't think he was doing anything untoward, (wanking). Which of course, they do. But, he kept going on about me wanting money.

"Bet you get lots of calls, don't you? Guys like paying you money. That's what you want, though, isn't it?"

Well, of course it is, I don't do it for the fun! Tosser!

He kept going on and on about how I like people giving me money and that I want lots of it and kept twittering rubbish about how I can't get enough money. It was like an obsession with him. He told me this one time there'd been a few other companies who never called him back.

By now, he was really starting to grate on me. A real slimy, smarmy voice he had. This is what he was like every time he came through. Never actually booked a call, mind. In the end to get rid, I told him if he didn't book a call I wouldn't answer the phone to him anymore. Well, that got rid of him for a while. A couple of months later he was back. By this time I'd forgotten his phone number so I answered the call. Amazingly, this time he booked a ten minute call. I rang him back, no reply. He never called back. A few weeks passed before he returned. I told him we owed him for a call, he said he'd had it. As you are fully aware by now, I'm the only one at my company. And this is how it went on. Then he came through and said I owed him calls. I told him point blank that he'd had the calls. I decided to play a little game of my own with the arsehole. Every time he came through to book a call, I let him drone on about guys not taking calls and how I love the fact I'm taking money off them for nothing, which is something I've never done. If for whatever reason I can't get through and they've not come back for a while I always remember, I write it down on their record card, same as if they've booked a call; I've done the chat with them. If I put the card through and it declines, I tell them when they next come through and it's sorted out.

So, back he came arguing the toss about these fucking calls. I told him that every time he came through wasting my time, bearing in mind he's on for about six or seven minutes, that's the equivalent of a ten minute call. My good paying regulars don't get it cheap, why the fuck should he. And I liked them! Anyway this finally put him off for quite some time. I got into a big argument with him and said every time he called my number I would deduct the cost of a ten minute call off his debit card. I still had his card details. At last, he's got it through his thick skull. Until the next time, Tosser!

Another craze that seems to be an obsession is blackmail. If you ever surf the internet there are hundreds of websites dedicated to guys being blackmailed. Piggy Slaves they're known as. Sometimes you get guys coming through on the call backs wanting to be blackmailed. They actually get a kick out of you taking money out of their account. I've got several guys that want me to do this.

For the main part most of the guys want to do it for real, yes they really want you to blackmail them and I do to a certain extent, I'm not quite vicious enough to go the whole hog but I can imagine it would be so easy to get really greedy. For some reason, I don't get a kick out of it. Oddly enough, that is important to me. If I don't enjoy the call, what's the point? I make plenty of money doing calls. Besides it takes up too much of my valuable time.

There is one guy I get through who does it just as a fantasy. He's only ever had me as Angie twenty-two and it's always for a twenty minute mobile costing twenty-eight pounds. I guess people might think that's a rip off but at least he's getting something in return. He gets off on the idea of me seducing men, getting them to their hotel room tying them up and then robbing them blind.

The fantasy always starts the same I'm in a hotel bar eyeing up my next victim. I saunter over to him, get him to give me money by saying a need a taxi to get home and can he spare fifty quid for the fare. Naturally, his wallet is in his room and I have to go back with him to get it. Then, me being the greedy bitch I am I spy his big wad of cash. I flirt with him then use my feminine wiles to get him naked. I tie him to the bed nick all his cash and leave him trussed up for the maid to find. This caller gets off on me pretending I'd do the same to him if we ever met up for real.

I suppose it could be argued I'm a con merchant doing what I do and that it still amounts to the same, conning a poor innocent victim out of his money and at the end of the day it's exactly the same as being blackmailed, relieving some bloke of his heavy load!

This one guy rings up to book a call with a Mistress. He came through wanting a young Mistress and Debbie is our young twenty-two year old. Anyway, he must have fallen for her because it's her he has all the time.

I always make him wait quite a while before I ring him back then I cut him off after just a few minutes. Poor old Tom can't get his head round it. I tell him, "It's what he wants. You don't understand that's how he wants to be treated." He won't have it; he reckons they won't come back, but hey presto. They come back. It is quite humorous, though.

"Can I have a call with Mistress Debbie, please Mistress." His little, weedy, pathetic voice comes crawling down the phone.

After assessing who he is, I tell him, of course he can. So, then, I make him wait not one, not two, but three hours. Debbie finally calls him.

"Hello, slave. Have I kept you waiting?" Sounding as if I don't care a shit and can't be arsed!

"Oh, that's okay, Mistress. It's just how it should be. It's what I deserve." He starts to gush and becomes a little too eager over the phone. I never say much to him, just grunt the odd reply. Once we were on the phone less than three minutes when I said.

"I can't be fucking arsed with you! You boring little wanker!" Then hung up. I could hear pleading with me as I slammed down the phone.

My man, Tom was absolutely gob smacked and shook his head in total disbelief when I told him what I'd done. "He won't be back," he kept saying.

Lo and behold, he's now a regular, obsessed with our Debbie.

One guy, who wanted to be blackmailed, actually lost his bottle after a while. It wasn't the taking of money out of his account, don't get me wrong I didn't do it often nor did I take much. Maybe twenty quid now and again. But the idea was, I'd send him a pair of my used panties and he would take a picture of himself wearing them on his head, his cock in his hand, posing in them.

By all accounts, he lives in this lodging house with three other lodgers. I got him to give me the landlady's name and the house phone number and address as he rings me on his mobile.

So, I duly sent off the panties with a lipstick kiss on the back of the envelope. Hoping it would cause some comment and to let him know I mean business. Oh it did that, all right. Never heard from him for two weeks, then out of the blue, he called and booked a call. Told the girl concerned, me that he'd moved and that he couldn't afford to call anymore. He was scared shitless. Little boys playing big boys games. Aren't they fucking pathetic? He obviously hadn't moved that's why he rang to say he had. Otherwise, why bother. Anyway, he gave me and Tom a good chuckle!

Not to worry, I still got my other little piggy slaves. The guy who comes through to book a call, and then doesn't take it. Not forgetting the little shit I hang up on. Oh yes, I forgot to mention the first guy I told you about. He still comes through. Still I shouldn't complain its money for old rope.

Chapter Seventeen

Mum's The Word

Why do some guys want to fuck their mothers? God knows! But, a quite a few of them do. If it's not their mothers it's their aunties, if it's not their aunties it's their sisters. The subject matter covers about a third of my regular callers. One of them has recently become a father, so his wife is now a mother, too. He still calls, but not as often as he used to. He can't I suppose while the wife's at home more. Mind you, he even called while his wife was still in hospital from having the sprog! Don't get me wrong, he's a lovely lad, really. Just a bit perverted, but aren't they all?

What is so staggering about this is most of the guys who call, sound in their forties or fifties. I do have a handful that are in their twenties to thirties, but it's not quite so common and it tends to be more about the auntie or sister. Also, the vast majority have, at some point, actually had sexual contact with said relative. I remember a caller came through one night, wanting to talk about his mother, but he wanted to be eight years old. From what he was telling me, I found it hard to believe from what he was saying, that he'd actually done the things he was talking about. That in fact his mother had really done those things to him, not just her but her boyfriend. It could've just been a vivid imagination, wild fantasies. I have to tell myself it goes on everywhere.

Incest, it's true what they jokingly say. Incest is okay as long as you keep it in the family. From the amount of calls I get, it must be rife.

Yes, we do get guys ringing wanting to talk about their daughters or nieces or just young girls in general. As long as they are not younger than thirteen I'm prepared to listen. Let's face it most teenagers lose their virginity earlier these days. I'm quite happy to talk about my early sexual experiences. I myself was sexually abused as a child so I do talk from experience. I only ever tell them the watered down version. But I won't talk about young kids. However, I am a firm believer in 'Those who talk about it don't do it'. And it's true; most kiddie fiddlers want to talk to kids, that's the whole point. They certainly ain't going to talk to an adult about it, that's not what they're about. Yes, you do get guys come on line and ask for young mothers, meaning they've got young kids. I always say, I don't know, you'd have to ask them yourself. It usually puts them off. I did have one guy come on who asked if I would be prepared to talk to a girl, a thirteen year old. I told him we do not talk to people under the age of sixteen.

Unfortunately, it does come with the territory. Guys want to talk about things they shouldn't, but you can't stop a guy from thinking things they shouldn't. That's just the way most guys are. In one way, I believe they should get something like that off their chest but at the same time, I don't want to encourage it. Keeping things like that bottled up can cause adverse effects. They want to get it out of their system. Most guys know it's wrong, some actually feel guilty and have said as much, but they can't stop those thoughts running through their heads. I can understand this. I've spoken to countless guys over the years about this subject matter. They do know it's wrong and being able to talk to someone about it does get rid of the undesirable yearnings they have for underage sex.

However, that being said, if it's something a guy really wants to do they will do it irrespective of what I or anyone else says. As I've said before, real kiddie fiddlers are only interested in kids. They wouldn't waste their time and certainly not their money on people like me.

I must add I'm not the only call back company that talks about underage, it's quite common. The other two companies I worked for both do.

The guy I spoke of at the start of this chapter, the one who'd recently become a father, told me from the start. "It's not that I want to have sex with my mother, God forbid. I want to think of you as my mother and that you're the one I want to have sex with." We always start with me, as his mum, catching him masturbating. I have to tell him it's the most natural thing in the world. It varies slightly, from time to time. However, the gist of it is always the same, me reassuring him that sex with his mother is the most natural thing in the world.

Most guys that come on it's the same thing. They even think themselves perverted wanting to talk about sex with a relative. This, of course, is how they want to be perceived. Some want to include their fathers in with the fantasy. The one thing always to remember it's just talk. Guys can't help what they think; it's sometimes out of their control. I suppose in some ways we are their confessor. It's something they want to get off their chest and that's what we're here for. Not that they want to do it, ever. It's just thoughts that run through their dirty minds.

As for the mother fantasy, I suppose it starts with puberty, it's the first woman's body they see. First erection, all adds to their first lustful feelings. You know how it goes, it's usually mother that catches them wanking and the little seed of imagination is planted. That's what it's all about really, something that happened in their childhood. Just about all perverted fantasies always start with something that happened to them or they've heard about. So, when they, like this first caller I'm talking about, starts explaining why they want to talk about what they do, I always say they same, I tell them not to worry. It's amazing how many guys talk about these things because they do. He himself when in his teenage years was told by a mate of his that he actually had sex with his mother. And the thought of this, this lad with his mother has been on his mind ever since. A great deal of these chats do have a source. Once you've discovered what that source is, it helps them with the sexual desire and it helps you to understand basically what it's all about.

It's like this guy, I have to tell him that it's okay, that it's the most natural thing in the world, boys wanting to fuck their mothers. Another thing he's obsessed with is his mother saying the 'C' word, as he puts it. And I say, "What, cunt?" It has the desired effect. Also, for some unknown reason, he likes to know he has his father's approval to have incestuous relations with his mum. What I do find a bit disconcerting is the fact he calls me mum when he books the call. However, since then I've had a new guy come to me and he has started to do the same, call me mum. I guess it all adds to the authenticity. It just seems so weird having these two guys call me mum. This second guy, this recent new addition to my stable, as Tom calls it. From what we talk about I think he at some point in his younger days has watched his mother with one of his many uncles. Now, of course, he recalls the memory and in the sick section of his mind it now turns him on. So much so he calls me three or four times a week to relive what he caught his mother doing. Except, now it's him shagging his dirty bitch mother (his words).

For the most part, guys who come through who want to talk to women in their sixties and above, want to talk to a mother type person. And, on occasion, their grandmother!

One guy I've got coming through, can't make up his mind who he wants to talk to, sometimes it's his mother, sometimes it's his auntie Helen. He's got a thing about catching her having sex, so much so, I think he must have caught her being shagged in reality. He wants her to ride his cock, the dirty old slut, as he calls her.

Another recent regular, wants an old granny type lady to use as a dirty old slut for his girlfriend. He, I'd guess is in his thirties, early thirties at that. Wants to dress her in short skirts, stockings and suspenders. Have big tits and wear low-cut tops. Wants her to have lots of sex with all kinds of men, and then lick her big hairy pussy clean. Yes, I know, disgusting bastards. What's that all about? And, if that's not enough, he wants to take her home to meet his mother for Sunday lunch. Why Sunday, who knows? Who of us knows anything!

He wants the old bitch and him to start foreplay at the dinner table then get me the dirty old slut, to sexually abuse his mother and make her have sex with her son. He wants to take us both to Jamaica, (don't ask!) and have sex with all the men who want to fuck us and then he will lick both our pussies clean.

Still, at least he knows what he wants and, at thirty quid a go, I make sure he gets it!

The one relative-related call that sticks in my mind, because as you can imagine, they sometimes do, was a guy I've only had a few times. He told me that he and his wife had parted, how lonely he was and that he'd had trouble coming to terms with it because he still loved her, but as he said, when they want someone else, what can you do about it? Anyway, he was getting used to being on his own, when his sister rang to say her and her husband were going through a bit of a sticky patch and could she stay for a few days. So, he thought why not, would be nice to have a bit of company and he hadn't seen her for a while. That first night, they both got quite drunk and snorted some coke. They really loosened up and chilled out. Both forgot their troubles. Anyway, she decided to go to bed and left him sitting on the floor, resting against the settee. He sat there finishing his drink, just thinking about things when, his sister appears in the doorway dressed in her nightie. By all accounts, she walked over to him, never said a word, took his glass out of his hand and proceeded to straddle his face. Apparently, she rode his face so hard that for a few minutes he could hardly breathe and was so wet he could barely swallow her juice quick enough. Then, she climbed off, knelt in front of him and sucked him off. Of course, it's turned him on so much the poor bastard can't stop thinking about it. When he woke the next day, she'd gone back to her husband and they've never spoken about it since. Whenever he thinks about what they got up to that night, he gets so horny, he has to talk to someone about it.

Thank God for the likes of me!

You'd think it stops there but it doesn't. Mother-in-laws, it's the same with them. I have this one regular who fantasies about his mother-in-law. He and his wife are staying with her mother for a while. She's off to work while her mother takes her son-in-law his early morning cuppa in bed. In she comes in just her dressing gown, nothing else. Of course, he's having his daily wank; she's almost got her tits hanging out. She tells him how lucky her daughter is having such a virile man in her life when she's no longer getting any. So, naturally, he obliges and gives her a good seeing to.

Aunties; they've got a lot to answer for, the effect they have on their young nephews; intentional or otherwise is unbelievable . Thankfully there's always me for the dirty little bastards to turn to.

For a recent caller that's been through a few times, it was a fantasy he'd done in reality. We do get quite a few of these, where something happened to them when they were quite young or even, on occasion in recent times and they wish to live out that fantasy. Again, as I've said before that's often where these fantasies are born out of, a real life incident.

The incident I'm about to recount took place for this caller at the age of fourteen. Apparently, he had a bit of a fancy for his Aunt. He was fascinated by her big breasts and the way she dressed and her perfume. All conspired to arouse the innocent teenager. One particular item of clothing which caused the strongest arousal was a coat of hers; a camel coat with a fur collar. One pretty similar to the coat Dot Cotton (Branning) wears in Eastenders, so he informed me. The sexual gratification from the coat was so overwhelming that on the odd occasions he was asked to go over on the pretence of doing odd jobs and so the aunt could tease him a little, knowing full well the effect she had on him, whenever she popped out to the shops or off license for refreshments he would put the coat on, and gleefully toss himself off.

Except, this one time she returned within ten minutes because she forgot her purse whereupon she discovered him in her coat, with of course, his cock out and absolutely rock hard. Well, by all accounts he was well endowed for a teenager, so how could a full blooded woman resist and apparently she couldn't and shagged him rigid for several months. Always in the coat. Then one time she rang him to come over and she'd bought a second coat and they wore one each while shagging each other senseless. So now, every time he comes through we talk about the coat and all the terrible sexy things she made him do. Yeah, I bet she had to twist his arm. Not!

Another guy I get who used to have my teenage girls now he only has me as his Auntie. He's always fourteen and I'm looking after him. Sometimes he wants me to tell him all the things I've done with my teenage son, starting with catching him masturbating for the first time and how I went about teaching and showing him the facts of life.

Sometimes he likes me to make him take his cock out in front of me and I'm so turned on by the size of it that get him to fuck me there and then.

One particular fantasy we did was where he was bullied and sexually abused by the boys at school. They were envious of his huge eleven inch cock. He comes home his clothes in disarray and I make him tell me all about it. Why he's in the state he's in and what took place. Of course he refuses because he's so embarrassed but I persist and force him to tell me. He does so eventually very hesitatingly. He tells me how he was raped by several of the boys. This again turns me on so much especially in the knowledge that my husband would love to enjoy a teenage boy. And, enjoy seeing me with a teenager. So then I have to go into graphic detail of what me and my husband do to him, mostly against his will.

The most amazing thing about the vast majority of these calls is the female concerned whether it be sister, aunt, mother or grandmother are the instigators, they are the ones who start it off. They approach the son, nephew, brother or grandson. Now the guy is older or the sexual relationship has stopped then the poor buggers have the uncontrollable urge to carry it on. That's why they call us week in week out. They start it and we, being me, have to help them finish themselves off and believe me I do!

It's a funny thing fantasy. What wild imaginings turn us on. Even at it's worst I have to tell myself it's just fantasy. But why do they seem to possess us so? A lot of guys talk about the same thing over and over and over again. It is an obsession. It builds and builds until finally they can find some release through talking to people like me. We are the only ones they can burden with something like this.

The guy I've just talked about thinks I know him better than anyone else. And, I guess I do. He was so convinced of this he wanted to get into a relationship with me. Like so many of them do. Because at the end of the day I do know them better than anyone else. I know their dirty secrets, their desires. I know what quite literally drives them to distraction. It's like it's a sickness and only I have the cure.

For the most part this is what it's all about, fantasising about what they shouldn't. It's an age old thing, one that guys just can't help. After all they are ruled by their cocks. God bless'em, that's what I say!

Chapter Eighteen

Cock Sucking Straight Guys

Yes, there's a lot of them about. I sometimes think it's the 'new' pussy. I get more straight guys wanting to talk about sucking cock than licking pussy. For most, though, drinking spunk out some dirty bitch's pussy will do it for them. Especially if it's their wife's. There's the odd few, and let's face it, there's a few of them about, want to talk about licking the spunk out of me after my boyfriend has fucked me. Then they go on to enquire if he'd let them suck him off.

"Oooh, would he!" I'll say. "And, boy, has he got a big fucking cock for you to suck. At least ten inches!" You can hear them over the phone reaching fever pitch at the thought of this.

Would he? What the fuck do you think! He's a bit of a kinky bastard himself, but that's where he'd draw the line. He'd be much happier to see them castrated! But, that is not the fantasy.

What is it with guys that they love the thought of being made to suck cock? A lot of guys come through wanting to talk about threesomes. Used to be me another girl and them. Now, it's me another guy and them.

"Would you like to see me suck another man's cock?" they start by asking.

"God, yes. That's fucking horny," is the expected reply. Then they go into great detail about sucking a man off, especially, after he's been inside my pussy and my arse.

The first time I did this sort of chat was with a bisexual, he wanted to talk about sharing a woman with his boyfriend. Wow, that was mind blowing; amazing. The thought of two cocks was good enough for me. He just went wild with his imagination and we had a real good time. The two guys sharing my pussy, he dripping his boyfriend's come into my mouth. Him teaching his boyfriend to lick pussy. He fucks me while his boyfriend fucked him. Him getting his boyfriend to drink his come out of me, while he licked his boyfriend's arse. The two of us sucking his boyfriend off. Then the boyfriend eating his spunk from my mouth. Oh, it all went on. I'm glad I had him come through when I did though, because that sort of three way sexual fantasy has become very popular. This of course, is why I'm now very good at it.

Another regular of mine, likes to think of me as his wife going out and getting fucked by loads of men, coming back with my knickers and pussy still full of their spunk. He loves to talk about me being home, fucking a few guys and then ringing up at work to tell him how much cock I've had up me and can he come home straight away because all that spunk is starting to run down my legs.

This is a very popular fantasy; I've got several regulars who share the same sexual fantasies.

How about the married guy who loves the thought of his wife making him suck cock? She's left him at home while she's out on the rampage. Comes back with a big black man, gets the guy to fuck her right in front of her husband. Then tells her husband to kneel in front of the guy and suck his big black cock. Then she has him lick out her cunt while the other guy fucks her. She follows this up by making her husband bend over and take the big black cock right up his arse!

Boy oh boy, do I have fun doing this sort of call. There's nothing better than getting a guy to spread his arse cheeks wide in readiness to be penetrated by some big bastard cock. What I love best is when the caller concerned is ramming a big fuck off dildo right up his backside! The sounds of moaning and groaning absolutely delights me. Ooh, the pain of it all. What a load of arse ache I must be the cause of!

Most of the cock suckers I talk to like to be dressed as a dirty slut, forced to suck cock. It's like it's part of their dirtiest perversion. Cock sucking being the lowest of the low. A straight man sucking cock. Occasionally, they want to be womanised to do it or they want to do it because they think it turns a woman on. It starts with, "Do you want to see me to suck cock?"

Another popular fantasy is me standing behind him and literally forcing his head on to the guy's cock. Making him gag on it. Bear in mind, although the fantasy of cock sucking is what they want, all they hear has come from my imagination.

Chapter Nineteen

Male Order, Bizarre Requests

You are probably aware that we girls sell our used panties. It's quite common, really. We can earn quite a bit of extra money this way. Well, I do now, working for myself. The first company I worked for gave you half what they charged. So, twenty quid got you any extra tenner. The second company paid you three quid whatever she charged. She always wore them herself provided the panties and paid for the postage. But now I keep all the money for myself.

They had to be worn for a couple of days. If they wanted a young girl's pair of panties, I usually shook a bit of talc into them. Maybe wore them for two days after I'd showered. The older the lady I was pretending to be the longer I wore them, the smellier they had to be. Guys are obsessed with girl's dirty knickers. I have guys who sniff not only their sister's knickers, but their mother's. Fuck, are men absolutely disgusting. I sometimes think who's worst? Them for thinking and in some cases actually doing it, or me? For listening and sometimes even encouraging them to do it!

Takes all sorts to make a world.

This is all well and good, really. But, you can get a bit bogged down by it all. This one poor bloke who has been a regular since all time. I actually mentioned him in my first chapter. His obsession is pissy knickers. He orders my panties quite often; he likes big ladies, which is handy really, because I am one. As I say, this has been going on for a year now. Every month or so he orders a pair of panties. Quite often there is a queue of guys waiting for panties and sometimes I forget, until they remind me. Regrettably, I forget his so often sometimes the poor guy has paid for his third pair before he receives his original order. I think, if I recall, I still owe him a pair or two.

As you can imagine, because I'm the only one doing all the calls it's very hard to go into town to replenish my supply of panties, they have to come in all colours and sizes. Tom works on a market on a Monday, so, this one time he offers to get some for me. I needed them for my old caller so it had to be big knickers. Size twenty-six. Well fuck knows what size he got me, they were twice the size of the ones I have and they looked like some old dear's knickers. As luck would have it my old caller always thought he was talking to different ladies of varying sizes. So, I thought, maybe I could get away with it. I put them on; they came up under my tits. When I saw this I thought, maybe I can't. In the end I had no other choice, so, I thought fuck it, and they will have to do. As it turns out, maybe they didn't do, I've not heard from him since!

He's one of my easy requests. Worn panties. Sometimes you get the odd request; they actually want you to piss in them. Some want everything, piss, shit and spunk. There's the odd one, a very odd one. He wants period blood, and shit on the panties. I remember this one time he'd ordered the panties in red and brown, if you get what I mean. So, I did the deed, when my monthly cycle came round. He calls me and asks if I've sent them off yet? Luckily, I hadn't. He had to go away for three weeks, unexpectedly. I thought, oh god, what do I do with the bloody knickers. You could say throw them and do him some fresh. If I wasn't going through the change I would've agreed. The thing was I didn't know when I'd be coming back on, again. It was just fortunate when he asked originally, I was on my periods.

I didn't know what to do; I'd already taken fifty quid out of his account for them. So, I rang my good friend Maria. "Oh for god's sake the dirty bastard. Put them in the freezer. Freeze them they'll keep for up to three months!" She had got no time for my perverts. Mind you she'd got no time for her own. She's the one who makes adult baby clothes for a living.

So, I did. One month later I defrosted them and then sent them off. He was a happy bunny, which saved the day and saved me from throwing away my bloody knickers!

Over the years some of us have had unusual requests. Normally, it's panties, bras, stockings and tights. Even on the odd occasion, worn slippers. It's not just the used sex toys or used condoms the contents of which are also requested. But chewed sweets, another chat girl I know from way back told me of the time one of her regulars wanted her to buy a pack of opal fruits. Chew them for a couple of minutes, then paid her five quid for each one. She has even had a guy send her the money for a pair of shoes. He wanted her to go out for a walk in them, step into some dog shit and send it off to him! I know it beggars belief. I thought this was the weirdest I'd ever heard of. It made my request sound quite tame. Until I had this guy come through who wanted to buy panties, tights, petticoat and toilet paper. Used toilet paper, he want three wads of toilet paper all with shit on as well as the panties. As you can imagine, when I told Tom, he said, "No! He's winding you up."

"That's not the best of it," I told him. "He's offered to pay me ten quid for each one!"

"Oh, No. You can't! Give him some fucking dog shit, the dirty bastard!"

All in all he spent a hundred and eight quid that day. Tom reckoned his card wouldn't go through, but it did!

Chapter Twenty

Time Wasters And Freebies

Oh my God! Time wasters! And, what a fucking waste of time they are! They go through all the performance of booking a call and their card doesn't go through. The best of it is they must know because they never call back to see where their call is. Or worse still, they go through the rigmarole of asking for details of all the girls and they just hang up.

Sometimes they come through and want to know the ins and outs of a duck's arse! And, when the same guys come through time and time again asking the same questions, still never booking a call, you could just about tear your hair out.

One particular guy springs to mind.

"Hello. Can I enquire about you prices, please?"

I'm sure he's putting a voice on. Like there's any need for a disguise.

So, I tell him.

"What girls do you have on at the minute?"

I tell him. Always the same answers to the same questions, and they have been for the last year!

"Do any of the girls sell their panties?"

Now, he wants to know all the types, sizes, colours and styles. Once upon a time I used to waste my time telling him all he wanted to know. In the end I just said no to everything he asked. Oh, don't worry it hasn't put him off. He still comes back from time to time!

Another guy I've spoken to umpteen times wants to know all the details, then says he can't book right now, he's got no money on his credit card. Then he starts waffling on about God knows what, by which time I've hung up on him. Why the fuck does he bother telling me. As if I'm fucking interested. Can't book a call, or guess what, don't fucking ring!

I told this one guy I'd had enough of, he was just asking a load of dumb questions about this that and the fucking other.

I asked his name he said Mr Somebody. I said Your name? Mr Whoever.

He was being a right arsehole, believe me you get a shit load of these tossers through. I was clearly frustrated with the arsehole. I said, is that what you want the girl to call you. He, of course, said yes. To this day, I can't quite work out if he was taking the piss or just thicker than pig shit. He was talking shit, I know that. Still I was getting no further forward. In the end I said, "Look, I'll tell you what I want you to do, you can take your mobile phone and shove it straight up your fucking arse. You tosser!" Amazingly, he never called back. Which, in a way, surprised me. Tom smiles sweetly, he's used to it, and gently enquires. "How's your anger management going, dear? All right?

"And you can fuck off, an' all! Does that answer your question?"

I wouldn't mind if it was a piss take or a wind up, half of these guys are really like it. I've got dozens who do it on a regular basis. I bet it's the same with all the other companies. I can't understand what they get from it. Abuse, usually. Nothing seems to deter them. One thing does put a vast majority off, asking for their credit card details. Their phone must be hotter than ours was on an extremely busy day.

One guy came through and asked for the girl he spoke last to. As you can imagine, I'm used to him by now. Now, I ask him for the name of the girl. Yes, he says with conviction. Her name's, Vanessa. At first, I used to say, sorry, we don't have a Vanessa working for us, or that he's never used us before. In the beginning I always thought he was a genuine caller, gave his details everything. But his card would never go through. So, as usual I put him down to being a time waster. Sometimes he'd ring, say he'd used us before, then wouldn't give his details because we'd already got them. So, in the end I just use to hang up on him. He even at one point threatened to report me to the Daily Paper we all advertise in. I'd got a few different ads in at the time and it must have confused the poor little arsehole. We got into a heated argument which ended with me slamming the phone down. He would just keep ringing back time and time again. I used to piss him off by not answering or leaving the phone engaged. One thing I learned from this tosser was that it was a response he was after, nothing more. This one I did get rid of. I just stopped answering the phone to him. I remembered his number and I smiled to myself every time it rang. There's nothing better than getting one up on some useless fucking waste of space!

I used to get this one guy come through.

"Can I have some details, please?" I gave him the details and he'd ask, "Do you do the calls?"

Of course, you get asked this many times. The answer is always in the affirmative.

I go to put his details through and, naturally, they don't go through. He'd say, "Can't we do the call, now?" Oh, yes. I'm full of fucking daft tricks like that. Do they actually think for one minute I'm going to talk about sex with them for free? Oh, I like nothing more than talking to some tosser for nothing. It's like, we do it for a living so we want to do it all the time. I actually used to get this one guy come through and say if I ever got bored, I could ring him! Are they fucking mental or what! I'd have to be to ring some tosser when I've got nothing better to do. You can imagine what my man Tom has to say. It absolutely beggars belief it really does!

Sometimes I play games with them, if it's a quiet night. If it's some twat on a roll, you get to know their phone numbers. I pick up the phone, but don't answer, or I ring off straight away. Then, I'll leave it for a while, listening to them saying, "Hello. Hello, is there anybody there?" Then I hang up. Sometimes I pick the phone up, of course, they don't answer. So, I wait for a while. Then maybe next time I start to chuckle, softly at first, so that they are not quite sure what they're hearing. Gradually, the chuckle gets louder, followed by laughing and if after this time they're still on the line I start screaming like some mad banshee. That does it. That finally does the trick, that finally gets rid of the little tosspots, they don't usually bother me anymore!

This last guy I'm going to tell you about is just one of those guys, the kind that beggars belief. Sometimes you get that pissed off at the same silly twats coming through you tell them the most ridiculous prices just so they fuck off. To which they say, "Oh I'll have to get back to you on that." Well, don't fucking rush back will you!

Anyway, this one guy was so persistent, ringing constantly, nothing seemed to put him off. Me screaming abuse, giving him high prices, hanging up on him. No matter what I did he kept calling back. I'm talking about a dozen times or more a night. Maybe, there's nowt on the box that night or maybe he's impotent and this is the only way he can get off. Finally, as a last resort, I passed the phone to Tom, "What?" he bellowed down the line. And 'What?' must have been enough because he never called back. But give it time, no doubt he won't disappoint us!

If all that's not bad enough, we have to contend with guys ringing up already having a toss. Well, it is only to be expected after all. But it's the shit they come out with.

You can hear the fuckers tossing off while asking for more details, I know them now, I'm ready for them, so I hang up. The cheek of them! They only ring back and say. "Oh, I'm sorry, I'm that excited at speaking to a girl, I've started already."

Yeah, right, of course. I believe owt, me. As if I'm as fucking stupid as you are. I'm not the cunt paying some bitch to bring me off, because I can't even have a wank without a woman to help me! They are, they're that fucking useless, they even need the help of a woman to toss off with!

Chapter Twenty One

Quick Off The Wrist And Boring Little Wankers

That's not quite what it's all about. Yes, there are a lot of them about. The worst or best of it, depending on whose point you're looking at it from, they most times book a fifteen or twenty minute call and they are done in less than ten.

I've got this one recent regular comes through, about three or four time a week, books a five minute mobile. We don't do a five minute landline, ten minutes is our shortest call to your landline. Anyway, he's usually gone in two. It's always the same chat usually with different girls. He asks for the most popular girl we've got on at that time in which ever age group that interests him that particular day.

I ask him, when I call him back, what turns him on. He never varies, blow jobs and hand jobs. My record with him is one minute and twenty-five seconds. However, the longest time it's taken is two minutes twenty seconds. He's one of the few guys who are easy and a pleasure to do. It's the easiest nine quid I'll ever earn!

There are quite a few guys just like this one. Another caller I've had since time began, only ever has a five minute call.

His fantasy is the same, forcing some young virgin to take his cock. He loves it when I tell him I'm a virgin and beg him not to touch me and how much I hate him for what he's doing. I'm a posh, spoilt little virgin and he loves the thought of deflowering me. For some reason it has to be on my birthday, my thirteenth birthday, and it's usually at the party. And when I start to cry, he's off and running, we've done the deed and I can get on to the next guy.

For the most part, it is only young lads who get off so quick. There is a small minority of older guys who don't go the distance. That's usually the guys who want to fantasise about young schoolgirls or big breasted women. And, you know what I'm like if they have a favourite word, what I call a trigger word, I play on it. And, blimey, Old Trigger is off at a gallop and they've run the race in record time.

Talking about schoolgirl fantasies I've got this one recent regular who asked for a schoolgirl fantasy, I gave him Sophie. For some reason I seem to do a soft sweet little timid voice for her. He booked a fifteen minute mobile which would have cost him twenty-three quid. He asked what I looked like and what I was wearing and that was that. I could hear him moan and groan at each description I gave, He was gone in about six minutes. I said to Tom, "Can't be bad can it?"

"Now, what?" he enquires.

"Twenty-three quid for six minutes work. There are all kinds of tossers but you can't beat the quick ones!"

However, what absolutely astounds me the most is guys who book fifteen or twenty minute calls and are gone in between five or ten minutes. The best of it is they always book the same amount of time every time they come through. Tom is always telling me to ease up on them a bit, otherwise they won't come back. It's not my fault they can't control themselves. Besides as soon as one tosser's gone there's another to take his place. Am I that good at getting them off? You betcha!

There is another type of quick call I must mention, the call that's interrupted. Quite often the poor bastard has just settled himself down to a nice little toss off, when the wife comes back or the boss has walked in or his girlfriend has just arrived back or his mate's knocking on the door. Sometimes all he has chance to say, is "I'll call the office." But most times the phone just goes dead. They always apologise when they come back, if they come back and say the reason why. I often wonder how close to getting caught he was or if indeed he did get caught.

I suppose what you have to bear in mind, before they actually ring us, they've probably been watching a dirty DVD or looking at some dirty magazines and we are the finishing touch, as it were. In fact they sometimes even tell us what they are doing, apart from the obvious, of course.

It's like this other quickie that often comes through, his obsession is big breasts and I do mean big breasts, like an 'H' cup. Naturally, I play on this fact and he's gone in minutes which is a bit wrong, but if I've got several calls backed up. Well, you know the rest.

For the most part, a lot of guys just can't hold it, well; they can hold it, but just not for very long. The funniest ones for me are the ones who have been and gone before you're even aware. I'm still on the phone doing the chat and they're off out the door with their hat and coat on, if you know what I mean. Bless them. Still, however long they need, it's all right with me, and after all they're still charged the same.

I really don't mind the ones who are quick off the wrist, they can be quite entertaining, for me. It's the boring bastards that do my head in. I wouldn't mind if they knew what they wanted, some don't even know what turns them on. If they don't then how on earth am I supposed to help them? Fuck me! They even think we're mind readers when it comes to their sexual fantasies.

The best boring wanker I have who comes through several times a week for ten minutes always asks the same, can he listen to a particular woman having sex. Sometimes it's an old bitch he wants other times it's a fat older woman, on occasion he wants to listen to me as Dee Dee having sex. So, there I lie grunting and groaning for three or four minutes, by which time I hear him say, "I've come, baby." And that's him done. He may even come back to me a couple more times in the day. And, God love him he's the easiest money I'll ever make. Yes, he's boring. Yes, he's quick but there's one thing for sure while there's guys like him around I'll never be poor.

So, bring on the quick little wankers, every boring last one. I need them to break up my otherwise boring long day. I know I do like to moan about them, but life would surely be boring without them!

Chapter Twenty Two

Virgin On The Ridiculous

Virgins, yes there are some still about. I've got three of them come through on a regular basis. A twenty-six year old I can understand. I actually had a twenty-six year old virgin when I was in my thirties. He was a body builder, fantastic body on him. Nice enough lad, on the whole. He was about to go into the navy, but didn't want to be a virgin. I know what you're thinking. Oh yes, that old flannel. Either way, I didn't mind, he was a good looking bloke and I had a free afternoon. I'd met him at his leaving party and my flat share girl introduced us. He asked her to ask me. Tell you what, never again! He was so nervous and he totally did not know what to do. Anyhow we managed it. He was no longer a virgin. Maybe this is why I so understand these three guys.

The twenty-six year old is quite normal in his sex chat, except he wants it to be with a sixty year old. I think what it is, is that they feel more at ease with someone experienced. A woman who knows what she wants and can take control because this is what you basically have to do. I must admit, in my own sex life I do like to take control, I actually like the shy guys. I like to make the first move. God alone knows what happened when I met Tom. I normally hate bossy, cocky guys who think they know it all, the big headed bastards, I don't usually give them house room. Underneath his gob, though, he's the best bloke I've ever known and we gel so well together. Not many guys would be tolerant of what I do for a living. I could be selling his plants over the phone instead of my fanny for all he cares. It's just a job that makes excellent money. As he has to work all the hours God sends to earn a living. All I do is lie on my back. As far as he's concerned, I've got it good. And I have.

The next virgin I want to tell you about is a thirty-five year old. He's the one I can be myself with. I try to explain to him how a woman smells and how she'd feel. He is so shy it's painful. His fantasy is seduction. The woman is to seduce him. I always think it's such a waste; him needing a woman in his life when there are so many women out there looking for a good man to love them. Yes, I know. I'm a bit of a softie underneath. But it's true, I've chatted for hours with this guy over the months. He is a genuinely shy nice guy.

We always starts the same, with my spying him in his local pub, then chatting him up before I whisk him off to my hotel. I lead him by the hand to my bedside. Kissing him, I push him onto the bed, where I tie him to the four poster bed, ripping his clothes off. Then I slowly undress, teasing him. I climb into the bed where upon I slowly devour him.

These calls are always such a pleasure to do, normal guys with the average sexual desires. Genuine guys who want to chat about oral, doggy style or straddling, boobs hang in their face. Sucking, licking and fucking. You just can't beat it. Unfortunately, there are not many of these about. I'd never get rich off these. I don't mind the healthy perversions or kinky sex. But the ones that set you thinking, well, there are loads of these about and they do make me rich. I suppose it's like most jobs, really, you have to take the rough with the smooth. However, if they are that rough, they give you nightmares. You can't just hang up!

My last virgin has an unusual obsession, unusual for virgins, not unusual for a lot of guys that come through. He's forty-eight years old, not only is he a virgin, he's obsessed about women going on holiday for big cock. Seemingly, when he's been abroad on holiday he has witnessed women hunting down the local men. Be it Turkey, Greece, the Caribbean, the Mediterranean, South Africa. In fact, any country where the men could be deemed to have big cock. So, I have to tease him something rotten.

"That's it, Martin," I tell him. "We can't help ourselves; we just love the feel of big cock stretching our pussy holes wide. On the flight over there, we get through three or four pairs of knickers we are that wet with anticipation at getting our pussies filled with big brown cock. Oh, and babe, believe me some of those fuckers are big, twelve to fourteen inches of thick meat pounding up us. As soon as we get there, we're on the hunt! Eager to find the biggest cock. We bend over, our skirts raised with knickers pulled to one side. We take cock after cock."

This is how the chat goes for twenty to thirty minutes. Sometimes we talk about our mothers in the war, how they used to take big American cock in exchange for stockings and chocolate, same principle, we're eager for cock. Of course the root of this is also why he's still a virgin; he's only got a three inch cock. I have to tease him about the size of it. Useless pathetic little wanker. Oh, and I say it with such feeling. I get it all off my chest! Right little toss pot.

Again, he such a nice bloke and I hate slagging him off but that's what does it for him. He likes the thought of me knocking the crap out of him because he's only got a little cock. He wants to be humiliated because he feels inadequate. Like so many other guys, he just feels inferior.

Chapter Twenty Three

Golden Showers, It never Rains When It Pours

It is far and away the most popular subject we cover. The next most popular request is hearing a girl pee in her loo! I mean, what's that all about. Does he stand outside his bog, at home, tossing off while he listens to his wife peeing? I'll bet he doesn't. Still, if a guy wants to pay me to take a pee in my own loo at home, who am I to deprive him? Some, a few, like to hear me take a dump! What's so horny about some bitch trying to shed a load is completely beyond me. I only know, the more I strain, the more he loves it.

No, I can't dump to order, but there are ways and means of making the caller think I am taking a dump.

Honestly, the amount of guys that come though and ask if the girl can have a pee for him is astounding. For the most part, I never disappoint. Quite often I'm desperate for a pee, anyway. Tom says, next time you take a dump, record it. Oh, believe me, I've tried, but it echoes too much.

Guys love it when they hear you say you want to pee in their mouths. The thing with talking about golden showers the fantasy hardly varies. Well, you can either pee in their mouths or on their cocks. Or they want to finger you while you're on the loo so you pee through their fingers. One guy wanted to pee up inside me. I told him I'd done it and it was very horny. It's like a fountain of pee gushing up inside me like having several guys spunking up you at once. This did it for him, that and the word, gushing. Another thing with guys who like talking about being peed on is you have to be hairy. A hairy, pissy fat twat. How sexy is that! Just as well really, because that's what I've got! Thank goodness I'm full of piss, better I think, than being full of shit. Although, on some days, I wish I was.

However, that's what I'm here for and I've got a lot of regulars who talk to me about it. Some guys do it, so they say. Some love to talk about it and wouldn't do it if their life depended on it. Again, it's dirty. The thought of it or actually doing it! It's dirty!

One guy, a regular from the beginning, comes through two or three times a month. He talks about me peeing on him, he likes large ladies. The larger the better. He buys knickers and pictures. Sometimes they are of me, not my face, naturally. Some I look for on the internet and once or twice I've scanned them from old dirty magazines of Tom's. He comes in very handy, I've got to say. Mind you he did start me up in the call backs; he paid for the advertising from the start. It took two to three months to start making enough money to keep myself and pay for the adverts and he, bless him, funded me, until I was in a position to take care of myself and pay him back, one day.

Back to the guy I've started to mention. Anyway, he's quite easy to do. He's had me as countless different girls. Always in their fifties, very large, hairy, fat pussies. The key words to get him off are, as you can imagine, fat, hairy, pissy lips. Big, fat, fuckable arse, gaping cunt. Thick, hairy bush. Repeat these words a few times and he's gone and I'm free for the next one. Sometimes it's handy to have guys you can get rid of fairly quickly, especially when I've got a few calls backed up. Luckily, all my regulars don't mind waiting, besides, it's more authentic if you tell them the girl they want to talk with is on a call. Usually, hopefully, they are prepared to wait. If they asked for someone else, I'm fucked, because there is no one else. I know it sounds like I must be mad doing it all myself. But without bragging, at least I'm certain the caller has a good call.

The most unusual call I've had to do with peeing, was this one guy who liked the thought of me desperate for a pee, but making me wait. That was a pretty cool fantasy. I must admit there are some fantasies I do enjoy, some that challenge me. I've always been good at thinking on my feet, been a great liar most of my life. Maybe that's where this writing malarkey comes from, used to making things up.

Anyway, I digress. This caller loves the thought of me being desperate to pee and only he can give me permission. I suppose it's what you'd call a submissive. Control over the other person.

He talked about me about what I liked. Got me to masturbate for him, which I'm happy to do, I'm happy to do it for most of my callers. He keeps asking every so often how I'm feeling, how desperate I am to pee. Is it starting to leak into my panties, yet? Because that's really what he wants me to do, pee my knickers. He wants me to be so close to peeing that he wants me to actually wet myself. Most of all he wants to hear me beg to use the bathroom. We go on like this for about five or six minutes. Only when I'm close to wetting myself does he let me go and the call then ends. All the time I have to describe what I'm doing and feeling. Crossing my legs, squeezing my thighs, gripping my pussy muscles. He sometimes asks me to tell him about the times when I was close, for real, like trying to put a key in the front door, or someone at the door or too far away from the loo. Told him about an actual time I was travelling along the motorway, and there were no toilets for about an hour and a half. How I kept rocking in the car seat, repeatedly squeezing my pussy lips together. How it was so bad I was actually in pain. I told him when I finally reached the toilet I'd practically wet my panties. He seemed to be very pleased with the chat. He's been back a few times, since. But thankfully, I don't have him as a regular. I don't think my poor bladder could take it. Just talking about it made me want to go to the loo!

This final guy into golden showers I want to talk about likes to tell me what he and his ex-wife get up to then we re-enact what they did. Now, this is most unusual for any fantasy. Yes, they want me to be their wife, but they don't actually get to do the fantasy for real.

As I said it's his ex-wife but they still get together for a bit of dirty sex. It's something they are both into and as yet neither has found a new partner into their little fetish. So, every time he's been with his ex-wife he likes to relive what the two have done.

He tells me where they've met up, usually in some hotel room. Tells me how she stood above him, raised her skirt to the tops of her stocking and pissed through her panties all over his chest and cock. How he's laid underneath her tossing his cock as she continues to pee all over his face. How he loves her to straddle his face so he can lick the pee drips from her hairy bush. Then he tells me he wants to do to me what he did to her. Then, this is where I continue the fantasy with him along the lines we've just talked about. He's a regular that has me as Dee Dee, the receptionist.

As I said early, it's easy to do the golden showers fantasy, because other than peeing over certain parts of the body there's nowhere else to go, really. Don't get me wrong each caller has his own slant on the fetish. So, no matter how many times I do it, it's never boring. But, then again, not many of my boys are. As Tom always says when a new guy comes through. "Another satisfied customer? Oh, good, anther one for the stable." And, I must admit, I do have a great collection of stallions in that stable!

216

Chapter Twenty Four

Different Companies And The Competition

We all do it from time to time, advertise under a different name. The name of our company has nothing to do with the ads we've placed in the daily newspaper or the men's magazines. I, myself have actually had four different ads in for my company, at one time. The reason; one ad appeals to one pervert and not another. Not only that, as Tom says you've got a one in four chance of a would-be caller answering your ad. To a certain extent he was correct. It got a bit silly though, when the same guy rang all four companies. He laughed, I fucking didn't! I'm the silly twat that had to keep answering the phone. Speaking to the same arsehole. Same time waster. Amazingly, you may be surprised to hear, there was the odd one that sussed us. Of course, I did change the details slightly. However, the most fantastic thing is I still get regulars from ads I've not placed for quite a few months. So, bless old Tom. He was on to a winner, after all.

My company name is an abbreviation of mine and Tom's surname. The last thing you want to do is make her indoors suspicious. Any type of telecom related business showing on your credit or debit card statement always raises questions if your spouse is the type to check out your card statements.

Naturally, there's a lot of card fraud about. It goes with the territory. Just recently I had this poor woman on, fraught because someone had copied down her husband's card details. I was a bit dubious, as you can imagine. But surely, there's no one low enough to get their wife to ring the call back company to get their money back! Anyway, the husband called, too. As soon as I heard his voice, I knew I'd never spoken to him. One advantage of doing all the calls. Apparently, I wasn't the only company this fraudster had done it to. However, I was the only one who was nice about it, the wife said as much. Why wouldn't I be? It's not their fault they'd been robbed. I told them I'd refund the money straight away, which I did. They were very pleased with that to say the least.

It's a regular occurrence; one company I worked for had a lot of this going on, at least every other month. Guys' claiming their money back off the credit card companies. Luckily, this year that I've been doing it, I've only had it done three times. One company reportedly went bankrupt because the mis-use had been going on for nearly two years. She had to pay all the monies back. How on earth can you not query a transaction for two years? The mind boggles.

It's as I say to guys who come on when they question the safety of their card details, there's only me that sees them. Because, there is only me! This is the main reason I won't take anybody on, I don't trust anyone. It's as simple as that. If my guys' cards are miss-used then it's me that gets it in the neck. And, quite frankly, I don't need to rob anybody. I make fantastic amounts of money at this game. In fact it's the other way round, callers owe me money. But that's the way the cookie crumbles.

What happens is, you're a regular caller, and you book a call. I've got a few calls backed up or sometimes, if it's early in the morning, I can't always be arsed to get out of my pit. So, I do the call, for whatever reason, without putting his details through. Occasionally, you're going to get stung. It goes without saying. Sometimes it's a genuine mistake, the guy will call at a later date to book a call. I explain what's happened and he's happy to cough up, if he doesn't, he doesn't get another call. Simple as that. For the most part, it is genuine. I'm pretty easy going, though I've done the odd call for free. Or I've let them run up a tab. One caller just recently paid off his tab for fifteen hundred quid. Oh, he runs up one every other month. He always pays it off. Then there's one guy who owes me six hundred, he got himself into a lot of debt, couldn't pay me. I told him not to worry about it. I'm not here to bankrupt anybody. It was one of those things; I shouldn't have let it go on for so long. He had spent a lot of money with me. So, what have I really lost, only my time? If the calls had been with a girl, I would have been out of pocket, then. I would have had to pay her, her wages. You just have to put it down to experience.

Another valid reason I do it all myself is the competition, and girls like me who start up their own company. A lot of companies get their girls to apply for work with another company. All the regulars and details she's given, she will pass to her original company. Oh, yes. They are always trying to stitch each other up. That's why occasionally, some new guy comes through and asks whether or not we send flyers out. Some companies send texts. No, I don't, I can't be arsed. Besides, I'm not that desperate for callers. Never have been. The second company I worked for did a lot of this, she'd get her main chat girl to log on with other companies and steal most of their callers. I gave her all the details of the guys I spoke to on the first company I worked for, she was a bitch anyway. Angela, her name was. The second company I worked for was one of her ex chat girls; they had a running battle from way back. Angela, even stitched one of her girls up with the benefits people.

That's what happens, most girls who work for these companies, are on benefits. I was very lucky, I had Tom to take care of me, and so she couldn't stitch me up. I myself was on benefits for a couple of months when I worked the premium rate lines. I stopped all that when my earnings took over my benefits. I suppose some people either get greedy or rely too much on state hand-outs, they can't break free. Not only that, if you're not very good at what you do when the calls and money start dropping off. They do live in the balance.

There is a lot of back stabbing and it is a cut throat business. When I started out, it was in fact thanks to the girl I last worked for. She advised me every step of the way, encouraged me, even. It was something I had thought about, Tom and I both thought it was an excellent idea. The money you can make in one day is astounding. My personal record for one day - don't forget it's just me doing the calls - is five hundred and thirty quid. It's nothing like that every day, it usually averages one hundred and seventy five quid a day, and that's every day of the month! The advertising costs around three hundred a month. I only advertise weekends and in the men's magazines, occasionally. The cost of calls, well, the landline calls I do are with BT broadband voice they are free and, the mobile deal I've got is two thousand minutes anytime, anywhere for a hundred quid a month. Another reason I do all my calls, I know they are getting the best calls I can give them and believe it or not, that is important to me.

So, now you can understand why it's so cut throat. There is so much money to be made, it's phenomenal. That's why I do the calls myself; no one can take them from me. If I've lost a guy for whatever reason I know it's down to me. Yes, I do lose a lot of callers, most often because they can't get through. However, while the world is full of perverts, my bank account will always be full of money.

Chapter Twenty Five

Me And My Regulars And Why I Love My Job

Yes, I know what you're saying, they are all my regulars. Yes, for the most part you are correct in your assumptions. But these guys are extra specially my regulars. These guys come through and have me as me, Dee Dee, the receptionist/owner. These are the guys who have been coming through for several months having other girls, until they give 'me' a go. After that they never go back to my other girls. Well, maybe the odd one, but they still talk to me, too.

Except this one guy, he always had me as me, Dee Dee. I sort of pinched him from my previous employer. I don't believe in filching other companies' callers, I don't have to. The reason why I did for this particular caller was every time he came through to book a call, I ended up doing him. Of course, as several different girls but that's what this game is all about. Quite often there's not many girls working for the companies so this is what they all do. I thought he might miss me because he was a fairly good regular, and that's why I told him. He seemed really keen to keep chatting with me so I'm glad I did. However, he had a very unusual obsession, his mother's backside. Fat, hairy and white. Apparently, he

222

caught a glimpse of it by accident when he was a very young lad and the vision has stayed with him since. When I told I had the same, he became hooked on me. That's how you hook most of them.

You can hook them in many ways. Another guy who's always had me is obsessed with the clitoris. God, don't we wish they all were!

The fantasy is centred around it, the clitty swollen and sticking out like a little cock. Say this to any guy and it sends him into a frenzy. He's always asking how wet and slippery it is and telling me to massage it. He wants me to take a picture of it all swollen and aroused, wants to hear me use a vibrator on it and make myself come. Then he wants me to put the phone down to it and let him hear how wet I am. I have to tell him how long I've been masturbating myself for and how many times I come in a night. Then I have to tell him about that certain call that's made my clitty really aroused and swollen. Then I have to tell him in quite graphic detail how turned on I am and how I loved to be licked out.

Basically, this is all we talk about over and over again. The chat never varies. Very easy man to please. I'd say his wife is a very lucky woman, if he's married that is.

Another guy I've had as Dee Dee has been calling since I've been working the call backs. I've never told him that I was leaving the company or where I'd be working but he always managed to find me. Guess this must mean I'm a big favourite of his. I do hope so, I do him three or four times every week!

It always starts with me asking him if he's got a big throbbing cock for me?

"It's rock hard. Could do with a nice wet cunt sliding down on it!"

"Mmmm, what you need is a couple of dirty bitches taking care of it."

This, for the main part, is the start of his fantasy. He's always wanting to talk about two dirty women and him , usually it's his girlfriend and me. The fantasy in itself is quite a common one. His fantasy though, is a particularly dirty one. The biggest turn on for him is his girlfriend who's totally against having sex with another woman and him having sex with another woman, for that matter. In actual fact he'd prefer it if I was a friend of his girlfriend's. You know, me staying over at their place and she catches him touching me up which of course makes her jealous. Oh, he loves this too, the thought of making her jealous. Even wants to go as far as telling her he prefers fucking me to her!

Sometimes we change it slightly and I maybe walk in on them having sex and I join in just messing around until it all gets out of hand and goes against his girlfriend's wishes but we've gone too far for her to stop it. Then basically he forces her to lick me out while he fucks her from behind. Or we go out for a meal, then on the way home in the taxi he starts touching the pair of us up. Well, we are dressed like a couple of dirty tarts!

We do several different versions of this same fantasy, it's all about him forcing his girlfriend into dirty sex with another woman.

A few times it's been me and him when we were younger. We are roughly the same age. I told him once, ages ago, about this lad I knew when I was thirteen years old and him fourteen and how when I'd gone round to see my mate from school and that her older brother always dragged me off to his bedroom where we would snog and do some petting, nothing serious. God, when I was thirteen we didn't know too much about the stuff the youngsters know today.

He would then tell me he wished he knew me when I was thirteen and him fourteen and that he would have loved to have taken me to his bedroom and licked out that sweet young pussy of mine and he would have made me suck his young schoolboy cock.

I don't mind this sort of underage chat as long as I'm the one we are talking about and I'm not younger than thirteen. I did actually get up to all sorts at that age. After all it's just natural curiosity between teenagers. It's when they are forced into something against their will or taken advantage of by someone who should know better that I strongly object to it.

I remember I told him when I was young girl how I always wanted to marry my father because he was quite a handsome man in his younger day and now how he's semi disabled. So then he wants to talk about me having oral sex with him.

He imagines me having to take care of him; dressing and bathing him and how he would get an erection from my touching him and me being such a good daughter I'd take care of it and give him a blow job.

How did this make me feel talking about giving my father a blow job? I didn't feel anything either way, I just thought of another man's cock I'd be sucking on and telling him in great, depraved gory detail what I was doing and how I was so enjoying it!

That's what I always do when they want me to do a call I don't really deep down want to talk about. Even when I'm talking about sex with another girl I just think about licking a chocolate based ice cream on a stick. It's the same way I turn myself on with most of my callers I imagine he's Johnny Depp. I could easily eat him inside out!

Thank God for imagination that's all I can say because believe me you need to have a good one!

It's why me for so many of my callers, they'll all say the same, it's my voice and they'll tell you it's as though I'm speaking from experience.

Some guys come through and like your voice straight off. They always ask the same, "Do you do the calls?" This of course, I always say I do. Most often it works to your advantage, other times, thankfully not often, it doesn't. Because you are the receptionist they seem to think this entitles them to a free chat. After all, you have been specially chosen for the chat with them. Yeah right, soft bitch's got nothing better to do. The best of it is, when they say after booking one chat with you is, if you get fed up or it goes quiet, you've got my number, give me a call. They must honestly think we are as dumb as them. They can't seem to get it into their thick skulls that we only do this for a living. If any girl does ring them back, then they are more stupid than the guys who invite them to ring in the first place!

I must admit, most times they can be very complimentary. And it is an addiction, hearing their praises. Even so, I'm only amiable to my regulars. They pay all the time, so I don't mind chatting with them every now and again.

A recent example is a guy I've had through several dozen times. Before, he's only ever spoken to different women at my company. This one particular time he came through and asked if he could speak to me. "Of course," I told him. Then added, "I'll put the phones on answer and call you back." We did this for a few times. Then he asked if he could give me his mobile number, so I could text him. I said, I couldn't promise to text him as we were so busy. I didn't want to say an outright, no, because I don't want to put him of completely. Two days later, he rang to ask why he's not received a text, yet. Cheeky bastard!

I said apologetically, "Sorry darling, I've been too busy."

So then, he asks for my mobile number.

"Sorry, don't give that information out."

He doesn't book a call, just fucks off. Which, I wish he would. The last few times he's booked a call, by the way, his card's not gone through. When he rings to see where his call is and I tell him the card's declined he says sorry and books again the next day. Without success, I might add. A few days later he's back and asks for my surname. With a curt reply I tell him that's not relevant information. Is he booking a call? Yes, he replies. Again, the bastard thing doesn't go through. Now, the last three days, I've just ignored his number when it shows up on my phone. See what I mean? Don't they just piss you off! I know I shouldn't, it's just that while he's calling he's preventing genuine callers coming through. Even to this day some six months down the line we are still going through the same performance.

That being said, even with all this agro going on it's still the best job to do. Best paid, that's for certain. The diversity of the caller and fantasy is quite remarkable. For the most part the callers are nice blokes, gentlemanly and polite. I love the friendly ones and the chatty ones. I love giving them the best time ever. I enjoy being able to do that for them, bring their fantasy to life, as it were. Help them get it off their chest, out of their system whatever it takes for them to carry on with their lives as normal.

Do I look at it as though I'm doing them some sort of service, I guess I must do. I just love hearing them say, it's better that sex! Guys do love to masturbate; it's as simple as that. It's got to be their most favourite past time. They get the horn in all sorts of weird places and oddest times. If they're on their own, what are they to do? They all think they're weird themselves, anyway. So they don't feel they can discuss it with anyone else. I guess I am perfect for the job.

Here in this book I have only given a small percentage of the calls I get, some are even more extreme than I dare give you. These last four years of doing this sort of work has been a complete eye opener for me as I hope it will be for you, the reader. All I know is it pays to keep an open mind in life and the vast majority of guys aren't really all that bad. They just possess wild dirty minds is all. Keep it fun and light and enjoy each other no matter what turns you on. Believe me there are worse out there than you've encountered in these pages.

How I do it day after day, night after night I will never know. It's not just getting them to toss off, if it was it would be absolutely boring. This game tests my imagination to the limit. I never fail to amaze myself! It's one thing to have to be a dozen different girls in the same age group. I also have to know how each one lost their virginity, first saw cock and first touched a cock. Or how dirty she's been. On the frequent occasions I've had to do one guy several times in succession, each girl has to have different desires, different tastes as well as guises. I am so there every time. It's all *ad lib*, for want of another word (or two). It just pours out of me, spilling down the phone through to their sexed up minds.

I must admit that it's only thanks to Tom that I understand men more, and all, (or most) of their perversions. Not that he's perverted, well, not too much. I did at first, think he was perverted, now I realise he's a normal guy with normal sexual desires and I do all I can to bring his desires to a sort of reality. You've got to remember my last husband thought

I was perverted because I wanted to experiment in bed with sex toys. He was absolutely horrified! If he knew me now.

I've always a bit of a dirty Girty. Always loved talking pure filth, working on Army and Air force bases, what else can you expect? Surrounded by blokes all the time, and getting paid for it. Well, what more can I say! I know I'm sick, but it's a kick hearing them come time and time again.

I know one thing for sure; it's something I'll be doing for a few more years to come. It's still as thrilling to me as it was in the beginning. It's never dull or boring, at least, not all the time. Really, I suppose it's like any other job in tele-communications. There are good days and bad days. Thankfully, with this job, it's only a caller at a time. So, bring them all on and I promise you a good time will be had by all. And for the first timer or non believer, don't knock it till you try it. So, why not let your first time be me? You never know, it could be the best twelve quid you've ever spent!

The End
(Or is it!)

You may also enjoy...

Uniform Behaviour

Edited by Lucy Felthouse

ISBN: 978-1-84989-662-7

A collection of erotic stories, each with its own unique uniform theme.

"A delicious electrifying pressure filled her body, forcing a cry from her throat before releasing a deluge of sticky sweetness. Sighing with pleasure as echoes of the orgasm reverberated through her, Philomena's eyes fluttered open to find Nathan leaning over her. There was a glint in his dark eyes as he studied her face, his smile widening before he dipped lower. As he held his body above her, his passionate kiss left her with a taste of her own juices. He smothered her with his mouth as she wrapped her arms around his neck, his solid posture remaining despite her attempt to pull him down onto her body. Instead, he pulled away from the kiss to gaze down at her."

Also from Cambridge House

The Dark Side of Maggie Moon

by Krys Antarakis

ISBN: 978-1-90747-584-9

An erotic novel featuring strong and intense BDSM-themed content.

Maggie is a successful career woman whose life is relatively calm and fulfilling until a mystery woman accosts her one day and suggests that she dress in a way that she finds scandalous. The mystery woman keeps on appearing and her suggestions become more and more extreme. But strangely enough Maggie finds herself drawn into following the woman's directions and they lead her into ways that are dark and mysterious indeed. Maggie is confronted with a part of her personality she never knew existed; her dark side. Pain and pleasure mingle for her in increasingly intense ways as she journeys farther into the dark.

Also from Cambridge House

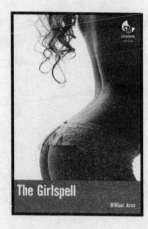

The Girlspell

by William Avon

ISBN: 978-1-90825-205-0

A cracking BDSM-themed novel from the well-known genre author.

"Gasping for breath she ducked around a thicket and crouched down, letting the riders gallop past. Before they could turn about she was off in the other direction. If she couldn't outrun them perhaps she could find somewhere to hide. But she had forgotten the Major and Platt. They thundered out from between the trees and rode straight at her. She leapt to one side but the Major caught her across the shoulder with his crop. She stumbled and fell heavily, winding herself and rolling over and over. Before she could recover her breath the whole party had surrounded her."